GATHERED IN HIS NAME

Devotions and Prayers for Christian Meetings

James F. Klawiter

CPH.
SAINT LOUIS

Published by Concordia Publishing House
3558 S. Jefferson Avenue, St. Louis, MO 63118-3968
Manufactured in the United States of America

Library of Congress Cataloging-in-Publication Data

1 2 3 4 5 6 7 8 9 10   08 07 06 05 04 03 02 01 00 99

CONTENTS

MEETINGS THROUGH THE YEAR

MEETINGS ON FAMILIAR TOPICS

INTRODUCTION

Where is the work of the Church done? It is correct to say that it is done in the hearts, lives, and activities of Christ's people. Wherever the redeemed are, there the work of the Church is done. The faithful carry out the command of Jesus to "make disciples of all nations" (Matthew 28:19) by teaching and baptizing.

The Great Commission of our Lord is a rule we can use to measure all other church activities. If the activity, whatever it is, does not in some way contribute to building up the faith and proclaiming the Gospel, its validity is to be questioned.

What about church meetings? Those ubiquitous gatherings of church people, be they large or small in number, fill many a square in church calendars. Let us agree at the outset that church meetings are a necessary part of the work in God's kingdom. The Bible is full of examples of meetings of God's people as they endeavored to carry on God's work.

From the first meeting ever recorded, the divine council in Genesis 1:26 where it was decided "to make man in Our image," to the last earthly meeting of the Master and His disciples on the Mount of Olives, where they heard the Great Commission, God has been a main participant.

Meetings will continue to be held until our victorious Lord suddenly adjourns the last one and returns in glory to assume the visible chairmanship of eternity.

Therefore, the purpose of this book is to help those who conduct church meetings to remember the Great Commission of Jesus and to ensure that in their meetings, whatever the agenda, the work of proclamation and edification goes on.

While paying lip service to the Great Commission, many church meetings soon depart from their spiritual moorings and drift into the waters of finance, policies, ways and means, and procedures. Many meetings begin with devotions gleaned from various sources, some not even spiritual in nature. Preparation for devotions is often forgotten, so at the last minute some religious-looking material is grabbed along with the hat and coat as the devotion leader hurries out the door.

How often is the Lord's Prayer hastily said at the end of a meeting? This is sometimes done while thoughts of the late hour, real or imagined insults, and additional work responsibilities crowd out thoughts of true church business.

This book attempts to offer the busy meeting leader devotions which are derived from Scripture and which zero in on the Great Commission. It hopes to bring to the gathering the sense that the Lord is also a member of group and indeed has something to say. It also contains prayers that may be offered at any time during the meeting.

Each devotion is based on a portion of Scripture and is applied to the unique needs of a Christian meeting. Hopefully our meetings are not so rushed that we cannot take the time to read the portion of Scripture with the devotion itself. Each devotion ends with a suitable prayer.

At the end of the book is an index, arranged according to topic, reference, and related subject areas, which should prove helpful in finding a devotion to fit a particular need.

Recall Jesus' words to Martha, who was burdened with serving while her sister Mary forgot the chores and sat listening to her Lord:

"One thing is needed," He said to Martha and He says to us. "And it will not be taken away from her," He adds (Luke 10:42). Don't allow the clock or the agenda to remove the "one thing needed" from your meetings.

My prayer is that this book will make more real the urgency of the work Christ gave us to do, and that in all of our meetings, He will be included as the Source and End of all we do and say.

James F. Klawiter

GREAT MEETINGS OF GENESIS

1 NEW BEGINNINGS

Read: Genesis 1:26–31

Then God said, "Let Us make man in Our image, in Our likeness, and let them rule over the fish of the sea, and the birds of the air, over the livestock, over all the earth, and over all the creatures that move along the ground." Genesis 1:26

Looking around the room, one can sense the excitement and anticipation as the new year's activities begin. People sit at attention, pencils, pens, and perhaps even laptops ready. Sheets of paper have been produced containing schedules, lists, procedures, and agendas. Great plans swirl through minds; perfect solutions await hatching and far-reaching programs are poised on mental launching pads.

Such was the occasion, but on a much higher plane of course, as the divine council's first recorded meeting is reported in Genesis. All was new, all was perfect, all was ready for the crowning creation—human beings! This was such a momentous event that the members of the Trinity actually used an action verb: "make." Previously, the operative phrase of the creation had been "Let there be …," but to create humans, the phrase used was "Let Us *make.*"

If this doesn't convince us of the importance of humans in God's plan, we should read on, noting the agenda that God has planned for humans. They are to rule His creation: fish, birds, livestock, and all creatures. Later God restates the list, adding, "Be fruitful and increase in number; fill the earth and subdue it" (Genesis 1:28). What an awesome responsibility, to be God's caretaker, God's second in command.

But the greatest news for us caretakers is that not only do we have God's power of attorney, we also have God's image. God gave our first parents His likeness, not in appearance but in actions. We had His ability to make only correct choices, just as He does. But we exchanged God's image for our own. Our own pride decided that we know better than God does—and this is called sin.

Sin ruined the optimism of the first meeting. Sin brought about a second emergency meeting where punishments were doled out, but more importantly, a divine rescue mission was begun. In Jesus Christ, a member of the divine council, we have a Savior who has restored to us the image of God—now faintly, but in eternity completely!

Look around the room at your fellow caretakers of God's kingdom. This part of the agenda never changed. We are all given the heavenly duty, not just to take care of the natural creation, but to care for and spread the Good News of the new creation, the Holy, Christian church. God could step in and do this job perfectly. Angels could do the same. But God has chosen us to further His work of sanctification.

It doesn't matter in what corner of the kingdom we have been placed or in what area of work we are found. God has chosen us to do His work, and this leads us to the original great gift now restored by Christ—God's image.

As this year's activities begin and the new work commences, admire, "ooh" and "ahh," congratulate each other, and then thank God as His image appears and reappears in the words and actions of our redeemed colleagues. As the year proceeds, the agendas lengthen, and the minutes pile up, may your group be a faithful image of the divine council, which first decided so long ago to "make man in Our image."

PRAYER: O Lord, come among us as we begin our work for You. Through Your Spirit, empower us to do the work You give us, as You would do it. Give our group the unity that You possess so perfectly. Open our eyes to see potential new areas to conquer for You.

According to Your will, give health and strength to all our members. Keep Satan and his allies far from us, that Your work can be done. Help us all to help each other in encouragement, enthusiasm, and example.

Hear us, Lord, because of the work done for us by Your Son, our Savior Jesus Christ, in whose name we pray. Amen.

2: AN UNFAIR CONTRACT

Read: Genesis 9:8–17

And God said, "This is the sign of the covenant I am making between Me and you and every living creature with you, a covenant for all generations to come: I have set My rainbow in the clouds, and it will be the sign of the covenant between Me and the earth." Genesis 9:12, 13

Of all the important meetings that are recorded in Scripture, this one might qualify as the most photogenic. Picture a barren and desolate landscape, trunks of dead trees protruding from pools of stagnant water. Dark clouds hover in the distance, punctuated at times with stabs of lightning. In the foreground stands an aged man surrounded by his wife, his three sons, and their wives. In frozen awe they stare at the brightness above them, hearing the words of God. Never again would there be such a meeting on this topic. These eight were the only people on the earth, the only link between life before the Flood and life afterward. Among these eight stood our ancient parents. What they were told, we are told; and what agreements they made, we live with today.

The topic under consideration was the status of creation. Noah and his family were no doubt as devastated in spirit as was the landscape around them. Among the many questions this meeting raised was: Would this terrible catastrophe ever happen again? Would the world become so overrun with sin that God would again have to scour it with another flood?

Then God put these concerns to rest. He made a promise to them and therefore to us. "Never again will all life be cut off by the waters of a flood; never again will there be a flood to destroy the earth," God said (Genesis 9:11). Could Noah and his family believe God? Can we believe God in this day and age?

To seal this promise, God displayed a miraculous sign—the rainbow—as a reminder of His promise never to destroy the earth again by a flood. But notice to whom the rainbow is directed. God continued, "Whenever I bring clouds over the earth and the rainbow appears in the clouds, *I will remember* My covenant between Me and you" (Genesis 9:14–15, emphasis added). God established this covenant sign for Himself. He is tying a string around His own finger.

God did the same thing when He ordered that blood be smeared on the doorposts of every Israelite home, a sign to remind the angel to "pass over." We live in safety under another sign when sin devastates our lives. This sign is the cross of Christ, reminding God that each horrible sin was paid for on that cross by His own Son.

God's covenant signs are all one-sided. The rainbow, the doorpost blood, and the cross all say, "God will not punish you because Someone else suffered that punishment for you." We only need to have faith—faith in what God says.

It is this one-sided promise-making that draws us together at this time, not a job we have to do, not requirements we have to satisfy, not a term we have to fill. We are not here primarily to quiet criticism, to keep bill collectors at bay, or to preserve our self-esteem. We are gathered here as a reaction to God's one-sided covenant of love, be it rainbow, blood, or cross. Our only motivation is God's love.

If God's love in Christ is not at the center of our purpose, we are no better than a business motivated by a bottom line. If the cross is not the rallying point for us, then our meetings are no better than social club gatherings where we are entertained and where we try to impress each other. If Jesus Christ is not the chairman of our board, we are working for the wrong company.

Did God keep His promise signified by the rainbow? Did He keep His promise smeared with doorpost blood? Did He keep His promise as presented by His Son on the cross?

Most emphatically, yes! And God's "yes" is what empowers our gathering, our congregation, and our faith. What a beautiful sign in a dark world!

PRAYER: Dearest Jesus, we give You thanks and praise for keeping Your promise to save us. How difficult it was for You to turn Your back on the glories of heaven, to carry our sins to the cross, and to die there in our place. For this we eternally thank You.

Motivate us now to be true keepers of the covenant in all we do and say. Put before us the vision of Your love that, through it, we can give it to others. Amen.

3. BUILDING BIGGER TOWERS

Read: Genesis 11:1–9

But the LORD came down to see the city and the tower that the men were building. Genesis 11:5

One of the most trying times a congregation or a family can go through is the time of remodeling, renovation, or building. It has been said that if a couple can endure a remodeling job, their marriage can endure most anything. The same is true of a congregation. With all of the decisions to be made, everyone seems to have an opinion and the mandate to express it. The building committee is deluged with ideas, some good, some not. Overall, it can certainly be a time of confusion.

Isn't it therefore refreshing to read about a group that was completely unified in a building project? Such a group was made up of the early inhabitants of the plain of Shinar. They found unity in their language and in their desire to defy the Lord's command to fill the whole earth. Unified in their means of staying together, they began to build a waterproof city of fired bricks and waterproof mortar so that any additional floods that God would send would not wipe them out. Besides these goals, the best one remained—they would make a name for themselves!

So they began building a city and, to top it all, a tower that would reach to heaven. They were planning to meet God eye-to-eye and nose-to-nose. God indeed took note of their attitude when He remarked, "If as one people speaking the same language they have begun to do this, then nothing they plan to do will be impossible for them" (Genesis 11:6). The seed of pride growing in human nature can produce just about anything. As evidence, look at what science is producing today, much of which eliminates a need for God.

In a bit of wry humor, God then announces that He would *come down* to see the city and the tower." Perhaps the divine magnifying glass would have to be used even to find it among the vastness of His created universe.

As we look at the city and tower that we are building at this meeting, these words of God will put things into perspective. First of all, is what we are building truly in accordance with God's plans for His kingdom? Or is it designed to do an end run around God's clear order? Or perhaps, as with those early builders, we are trying to build a name for ourselves. What is God's opinion as He stoops to examine what we are doing?

Second, if what we are building is according to God's plan and with His blessing, perhaps we need to see our project next to the one God is doing. No matter how important our project is to us, how demanding it is of our talents and treasures, it shrinks into insignificance when measured next to God's greatest work—salvation. How can we even think of putting our plans on the same table with God's masterpiece of eternal redemption?

Finally, as we begin our work, would it not be wise to enlist the direction and help of Him who designed and built all things? Would it not be the wisest of plans to make sure that what we do fits into God's master plan? Then God's coming down to see what we are doing will be a welcome inspection.

PRAYER: Dear Lord, we ask for Your presence among us as we plan and build for You. Guide our decisions to fit into Your master plan. Help us be willing workers to make Your name glorious. In Jesus' name. Amen.

4 LEGAL DISHONESTY

Read: Genesis 12:10–20

[And Abram said,] "When the Egyptians see you, they will say, 'This is his wife.' Then they will kill me but will let you live. Say you are my sister, so that I will be treated well for your sake and my life will be spared because of you." Genesis 12:12, 13

The text for this devotion is not exactly a meeting. Rather, it is a private conversation between a husband and his wife as they face a life-threatening situation.

The situation might be somewhat foreign to us, but it certainly was not to Abram. He and his household had moved to Egypt to escape a famine in Canaan. The danger came because of Sarai's beauty. She certainly would be noticed by Pharaoh, and, as was the custom then, she would be taken into his harem. Her husband would be considered a rival and would be killed.

Abram's plan was to lie. When questioned, he would say that Sarai was his sister. This would solve his problem—he would be spared—but it certainly wouldn't solve Sarai's problem. She would be taken into the royal harem and we can imagine the rest of the story.

This is exactly what happened. However, God stepped in to correct what Abram apparently could not see. God afflicted the royal court and its holdings with serious diseases. Pharaoh figured out why this was happening, called Abram in, accused him of lying, and then sent Abram and Sarai on their way.

One does not hear this story read or used as a text for sermons very often, probably because it reports a serious sin done by one of the Old Testament's great heroes of faith. God included it in the sacred record, as Paul says, "to teach us" (Romans 15:4). What can we learn from it?

We are all sinners, individually and collectively. The fact that this group is working for the church does not exclude it from sin. Indeed, many church groups are responsible for sins that make secular organizations cringe: embezzlement, tax evasion, slander, even copyright infringement. For a more detailed list, read Paul's first letter to the Corinthians. God's people, individually or collectively, are not immune from sin.

What is so sad, as it was with Abram, is that many of these sins are committed with what we think is a noble purpose: "Spare Abram's life." "Divert tax money for missions." "Remove an unpopular pastor through a grassroots whispering campaign." "Provide worship music without paying for it with the help of the copy machine."

Like Abram, we don't see the ominous tentacles of grief caused by our "noble sins." Poor Sarai would be reduced to the status of a kept woman. A congregation would be laughed at as it is publicly ordered to make good on its tax obligation. Not only would a pastor's reputation be ruined as he is removed from office, but Satan would have free reign in a shepherdless congregation. How pleasing to God are praises sung from music that is stolen? Sin, no matter who does it, leaves behind a dreadful mess.

God does step in and correct the problem, just as He did with Abram. However, God doesn't suddenly appear at a congregation meeting and force a 180 degree change in direction. What God does is place before us a hill with a cross on it, bearing the body of one who is labeled embezzler, liar, cheat, adulterer, thief! His own Son is the corporate substitute for our "noble sins." Jesus died in agony, not from noble sins, but from sins that kill.

His sacrifice now enables us to live and conduct

business in a straight line. No lies, no end runs, and no cover-ups are necessary. Faith in God, who does all this for us, dictates policies that are what God would do—and did!

PRAYER: O Lord, our heavenly Father, we ask Your forgiveness for the times that we made expedient what You consider wrong. For the sake of Your suffering Son, pardon us individually and collectively for our misuse of our roles in doing Your business. Teach us to step forward boldly, doing the right thing, even though the wrong seems more expedient. In Jesus' name we pray. Amen.

5 SPLITTING UP IS HARD TO DO

Read: Genesis 13:5–18

So Abram said to Lot, "Let's not have any quarreling between you and me, or between your herdsmen and mine, for we are brothers. Is not the whole land before you? Let's part company. If you go to the left, I'll go to the right; if you go to the right, I'll go to the left."
Genesis 13:8, 9

This meeting between Abram and his nephew, Lot, is among the most famous meetings in the Bible. God had so blessed the flocks of both Abram and Lot that they were running out of pastureland. Not surprisingly, quarrels between herdsmen over grazing and water rights began to erupt.

At this point we might expect a full-blown two-hour mini-series to result. Imagine what the Hollywood writers could do with this situation. Good, old, righteous Abram is being harassed by his young, upstart nephew, Lot. Lot, with his greater knowledge of technology and an utter disregard for family values, begins taking over his uncle's vast holdings. Of course, the writers would have to inject some intrigue between Sarai (Abram's wife) and Lot and/or Lot's wife. They might even make a reference to a pile of salt, to be more authentic. Who knows (or cares) how this version would end?

But God's version would never sell, mostly because it is a true account and true to the life of believers. The upshot is that when a serious problem arose, Abram and Lot had a meeting. During this meeting Abram showed his faith and love for the Lord. First, he saw that to do nothing would make the problem worse. The obvious course was to split up.

The wisdom and love of God is seen not in the decision to split the land, but in how the land was split. Abram, who was given the entire land, told Lot, "You have first choice. If you go left, I'll go right. If you go right, I'll go left." How could Abram afford to be so generous?

His generosity was nothing more than God rubbing off on him. Abram remembered how God had blessed him in his journey from Ur of the Chaldees to Canaan and how God had protected him even when Abram didn't deserve it. (See the incident in Genesis 12.) Above all was God's promise, "Through you, all nations will be blessed" (See Genesis 12:2–3). With all of these gifts, why should Abram be concerned if Lot had the first choice?

We can learn from Abram. God has given us even more to prove His love than He gave Abram. Abram could only look forward to Him through whom all nations are blessed. We are the nations who have been blessed though Christ. Abram had only infrequent messages from God. God has given us a daily memo from His Word to guide and sustain us. Abram had only his wife and servants to support him in a hostile land. We have the warmth and support of fellow Christians who gather with us weekly and strengthen us in our faith. Who do you think is in a better position to be generous?

Many meetings that we attend have at their root the subject of who is being taken advantage of and who is being unfair. The issue may be buried beneath a pile of reports and motions, but it is there nonetheless. What an exercise in faith it would be if those who are in control would give in to those whose methods seem different! What an example of generosity it would be if young and old alike would agree to control their tempers for a time. And so we follow God's clear directions for us in Scripture and can use the decisions of our meetings to demonstrate God's generosity to us.

Splitting up is hard to do. Giving in is even harder. But when we recognize the loving, supporting hand of God beneath us, we realize we haven't given up anything.

PRAYER: Dear Father in heaven, as we gather to do Your business, fill us with Your Spirit and a measure of Your generosity. Open our eyes to see other points of view. Remove from the discussion the minefield of personal conflict. Help us see the wider vision of work to be done for You and not just for ourselves. Make us truly one in Christ, who truly made us one with You. Amen.

6 ON BEING HARD-NOSED

Read: Genesis 18:16–33

*Then he [Abraham] said, "May the L*ORD* not be angry, but let me speak just once more. What if only ten can be found there?"*

He [God] answered, "For the sake of ten, I will not destroy it."
Genesis 18:32

We've all been there: haggling in the little office in the new car showroom, talking to the proprietor of the second-hand shop, listening to the voice on the phone which has an offer too good to pass up. We've had our share of bargaining sessions—some successful, some not. Some people bargain well, others don't. Some are more interested in winning a battle of wits than in talking about the potential deal.

Abraham, the father of believers, found himself in a difficult position. His nephew, Lot, had become a full-time citizen of Sodom—a spiritual sewer of Canaan. God had just announced that the cities of Sodom and Gomorrah were to be destroyed. What should Abraham do about Lot and his family?

Saving or destroying cities was God's concern. Abraham's concern was for his nephew. Would God actually destroy Lot and his family along with the evildoers of Sodom and Gomorrah? God could do what He wanted and could have told Abraham to stay out of it.

Yet God thought enough of Abraham to tell him His plans and to listen as Abraham took the leap of faith by bringing up the matter. "Will You sweep away the righteous with the wicked?" Abraham asked (Genesis 18:23). What he meant was, "God, You are righteous and perfectly just. How, therefore, could You destroy those who are also righteous (Lot and family)? Is that just?"

God could have said, "Mind your own business, Abraham! My mind is made up. The city goes!" He could have said, "Let Me think about it. I'll get back to you later." But He didn't. He said that for the sake of fifty He wouldn't destroy it, answering, "If I find fifty righteous people in the city ... I will spare the whole place for their sake" (Genesis 18:26).

God's answer did three things. It showed Abraham that God loathed sin and would punish those who persisted in it. At the same time, it showed that He loved His people enough to do what it took to nurture their faith. Finally, it encouraged Abraham to try again.

Abraham did so. He went from 50 to 45, to 40, to 30, to 20, and finally to 10. Each time Abraham stepped a little closer to the edge. How far could he go with his bargaining? God could have turned him off 40 people back, but He didn't. God encouraged Abraham to plead, to bargain, and to pray.

When St. Paul wrote in 1 Thessalonians 5:17, "Pray continually," this is what he had in mind. If God does not answer either yes or no, then God's intention is that we continue praying. If God's answers are always yes, we become spiritual couch potatoes. If they are always no, we look elsewhere for our good. So sometimes God says nothing, thereby encouraging us to keep praying.

What is true for individuals is also true for groups. The goals seem to get farther away, the contributions down, apathy up, the call returned, the permit delayed. Rather than being stop signs, God would have us read these obstacles as "pray signs."

In business it is called being persistent, pushy, or hard-nosed. In God's business it is called being God-hearted!

PRAYER: Dear Lord, thank You for the seeming obstacles that You place in our way. Thank You for the example of Abraham and his persistence in prayer. Give us that same spirit that we might persevere in our prayers, never giving up until Your will is done. According to Your will, give us the answers we need and keep us close to You. In Jesus' name. Amen.

7 BAD BUSINESS FOR GOOD PEOPLE

Read: Genesis 23:1–19

He [Abraham] said, "I am an alien and a stranger among you. Sell me some property for a burial site here so I can bury my dead."
Genesis 23:4

No one wants to be in a no-win situation, when an emergency business arrangement gives the other party all the advantages.

This was the position that the aged Abraham was in as he made burial arrangements for his beloved Sarah. He was in a foreign land; he owned no property, even though God had said the entire land was his. Now Abraham had to buy some land quickly for a burial site.

His dealings were with Ephron, a Hittite chief who owned the property in question. Ephron's first answer to Abraham's offer was too good to be true. In the presence of all the town elders he said, "Listen to me; I give you the field, and I give you the cave that is in it" (Genesis 23:11). Abraham refused, again offering to pay the full price. Why?

If Abraham had accepted Ephron's "gift," Sarah's burial spot would, in effect, still belong to Ephron. Abraham wanted some property that was truly his, paid for, not dependent upon someone else's whim. It was his first investment in the land God had promised him. So Abraham offered to pay the full price.

Reading on, we find that Ephron not only extorted an inflated price (400 shekels of silver) but that it was not even standard weight; it was determined by the local merchants. Abraham was in a tight spot. He knew he was being taken advantage of, but he chose to give in.

We would say it was bad business, but Abraham would say, "So be it!" Abraham was no business novice, being recognized in Canaan as a man of great wealth and prestige. Yet he accepted a bad deal because of another trait he had—faith. The writer of Hebrews explained it this way, "For he [Abraham] was looking forward to the city with foundations, whose architect and builder is God" (Hebrews 11:10).

Abraham was ready to make a monetary investment in a deal that would result in a spiritual payoff. He was willing to be taken advantage of so God's work could be carried on into eternity. Providing Abraham's offspring with the entire land of Canaan was just a small part of God's greater plan. From this emerging nation came the Savior of the world.

God does not want, and indeed rejects, our misuse of earthly resources. Poor stewardship of God's resources is never acceptable, nor do we relish being taken advantage of in the business of the church. But when we must choose between monetary gain or spiritual gain, we have only one choice. We will accept a bad business deal if it is a gain for God's kingdom.

Look at what God paid to buy us back from sin. "Not with ... silver or gold ... but with the precious blood of Christ" (1 Peter 1:18–19). This was one "bad" deal that gives us joy into eternity.

We are therefore encouraged to look at the church's business from heaven's front office view. Money invested in evangelism won't bring in profit, but, God willing, it does bring in people for His kingdom. A tithe of church offerings for missions might produce red ink but will result in covering millions with the cleansing red blood of Jesus. Pledges and offerings for expanded worship and education facilities might exhaust the congregation, but they certainly strengthen the faith and trust level of the members.

Abraham is called "the father of believers" for good reason. His belief in what God was doing was greater than his business sense. We pray that we are "like father, like children."

PRAYER: Dear Lord and Father of us all, we pray that, as Your Spirit moves in us, we may be moved to look beyond bottom lines and ink color. Enable us to see the larger opportunities that we have for making investments in Your kingdom. Remove from us the fear of earthly failure, and fill us with the joy of spiritual adventure. Hear us, Lord, for the sake of Jesus our Savior. Amen.

8 ON MAKING THE BEST DEAL

Read: Genesis 29:14b–30

Laban said to him, "Just because you are a relative of mine, should you work for me for nothing? Tell me what your wages should be ..."

Jacob was in love with Rachel and said, "I'll work for you seven years in return for your younger daughter Rachel."
Genesis 29:15, 18

Get out the picket signs. Call the TV stations. Hold a news conference. There's going to be a strike! When people are unhappy with their wages, working conditions, or benefits, one way to deal with it is to stop working until the demands are met. The two opposing sides, employer and employee, are forced to negotiate, and what begins as a discussion over issues can deteriorate into arguments involving personalities.

Two of the most unlikely personalities ever to have a meeting over wages were Jacob and Laban. Laban was the brother of Jacob's mother, Rebekah, and master of the household of Bethuel of Aram. He was the master of the slick deal, the employer who promised the moon and delivered a hunk of moldy cheese.

Jacob, although younger, was probably Laban's equal in craftiness. His name in the modern idiom could be translated as "Pushy." He swindled his brother, Esau, out of his birthright and blessing, and then came to stay with his uncle because Esau had vowed to kill him.

Now the two masters of the art of swindle faced each other. On the surface they seemed to make a fair deal. Jacob would work seven years for Laban's daughter, Rachel, the love of Jacob's life.

But in hearing the rest of the story, we find that Laban deceived Jacob. At the last minute, he switched his eldest daughter, Leah, for Rachel, and Jacob unwittingly became the husband of a girl he didn't love. Laban explained that in Aram, the eldest daughter was always married first. Jacob promised to work seven more years for Rachel. He therefore ended up with two wives and another seven years of hard labor. Laban, it seems, won this round.

Satan is our unseen Uncle Laban. He would like to use us as Laban used Jacob and his craftiness is well-documented. He first deceived Adam and Eve, promising them an expanded view of life but delivering only death. He used righteous Job as a laboratory specimen to demonstrate to God how fickle a human can be, and Job lost family, possessions, and health as a result. Satan's trail of unfair deals extends through the Old Testament, New Testament, and into the present.

Even though he was put out of business permanently at Calvary, Satan continues to have "going-out-of-business sales." His biggest lie to us is that he still owns us. As his time runs short, he works even more diligently to deceive all who will listen to him.

The church seems to be listening. In an attempt to be attractive and relevant, it has "dumbed down" the clear message of sin and grace and created a caricature of Jesus Christ who is everyone's friend but nobody's Savior. It now features ministers who use the sermon to entertain and enlighten, but who do not speak God's Word. This all bears the fingerprints of Satan, who promises what we want and withholds what we need. His intent is to produce happy people who don't have a clue about their eternal destiny. They willingly follow a counterfeit Jesus and march steadily and happily into hell. Such is Satan's deal.

But God has provided for us the true Master of the

deal, Jesus Christ. He demonstrated how to defeat this slick serpent by using a weapon Satan cannot defeat— God's Word. Our true mission is to proclaim that Word truthfully and completely to all people. No trade-offs, no compromises, no under-the-table deals. We proclaim Jesus Christ, divine Savior, divine Master of our souls.

Jacob and Laban slugged it out for 21 years. God has ended the bargaining—Satan is out. Grace through Jesus Christ is in. The contract is forever.

PRAYER: Eternal Savior, thank You for exposing Satan as he is—the father of lies. Thank You for demonstrating the power of Your Word over him and crushing him at Calvary, freeing us from his demands. We praise You for this victory and for the free gift of life forever with You. Amen.

9 IT ISN'T WHAT YOU THINK

Read: Genesis 31:43–55

[And Laban said,] "Come now, let's make a covenant, you and I, and let it serve as a witness between us. ... May the LORD keep watch between you and me when we are away from each other."
Genesis 31:44, 49

The dull, gray pod hangs limply from a branch, having no sign of life, but in the gentle warmth of spring, the chrysalis breaks open and out emerges a beautiful butterfly. The shiny, green leaves of a plant hidden in the underbrush, when touched, will produce a rash that will end summer fun. Such is the legacy of poison ivy. The shiny, used car sitting in the driveway gives its teenage owner the promise of many adventure-filled evenings. The promise soon becomes a burden as bills for gas, insurance, and upkeep begin to mount. Surface appearances don't always disclose what is underneath.

One of the most often used passages from the Old Testament is the Mizpah Blessing: "The LORD watch between me and thee, when we are absent one from another" (Genesis 31:49 KJV). It projects the beautiful scene of God shielding two friends from harm and danger while they are parted. The purpose of this meditation is not to destroy that beautiful image. Out of context, the fact that God watches and cares for parted friends is quite scriptural and very comforting.

The hard fact of the matter is that this blessing was really no blessing at all. It was a threat issued by the sly Laban to his opportunistic nephew, Jacob. Jacob had fled from his uncle's estate with two of Laban's daughters, eleven grandsons, one granddaughter, numerous servants, and countless livestock. Laban had pursued Jacob, intending to bring him, or at least his possessions, back. But God intervened, telling Laban, "Be careful not to say anything to Jacob, either good or bad" (Genesis 31:24).

As a result, Laban suggested piling up rocks as a reminder of the mistrust that each had for the other. In Laban's thinking, that pile of rocks was a symbol of the Lord keeping watch between himself and Jacob so neither of them would sneak around trying to "get" the other. Such a monument hardly held a beautiful sentiment of two loving friends.

We might call our monument a code of ethics, an operations manual, or a policy paper. In church work we might call it a handbook, by-laws, or a job description. These documents, in or out of the church, serve the same purpose—to direct behavior. We are calling upon a pile of paper to be our Mizpah.

To be sure, good order and stewardship require clearly stated and understood procedures. God's blessings also come along with careful planning and foresight. But when all we erect is a pile of paper, complete with built-in safeguards, non-escape clauses, and irrevocable articles, we are in danger of forgetting the purpose of these documents.

The work of the Lord for His kingdom is built upon Jesus Christ and His death and resurrection for us. We are all recipients of this massive load of grace. We are all motivated by His Spirit to do the best we can for Him.

We therefore understand that "Christ's love compels us, because we are convinced that one died for all ... that those who live should no longer live for themselves but for Him who died for them and was raised again" (2 Corinthians 5:14, 15).

Do we need a paper pile to make sure we behave? Do we need a club made of rules and regulations to get

Christ's work done? Is a job description the prime motivator of what we do? In answer, listen again to the adjusted Mizpah Blessing, but this time using the cross of Christ as the monument: "May the Lord Jesus keep watch over us as we are absent from Him but continue His work together."

PRAYER: Lord Jesus, come into our group with Your peace and blessing, filling our hearts with a renewed desire to please You and to do Your work. Help each of us to help each other to do the best we can. Keep watch over us until we come to Your home where we can keep watch with You. Amen.

ELIMINATING THE DREAMERS

Read: Genesis 37:17b–28

But they saw him in the distance, and before he reached them, they plotted to kill him. "Here comes that dreamer!" they said to each other. "Come now, let's kill him ..." Genesis 37:18, 19

Think of a person who walks through life hearing a different beat, whose style is out of sync with everyone else, who zigs while others zag, who seems to be attached to the earth only by gravity. In terms of this text, a dreamer.

Joseph fit that description to a "tee." Besides having a different mother, the ten sons of Jacob resented him for a number of reasons. He tattled on them when they did wrong. He was obviously his father's favorite as he sported a coat worn only by the leisure class. To top all of that, he had the nerve to tell them his dreams and that they would all bow before him some day.

The story of how Joseph's brothers disposed of him and how God used Joseph to further His plan is one of the more interesting in Scripture. Let our attention be focused on this quick emergency meeting, where the brothers hatched their ill-conceived plan to eliminate their brother, the dreamer.

Like Joseph's brothers, the Bible is full of others who plotted to dispose of dreamers. Particularly we think of the enemies of Jesus. The Pharisees and Sadducees could agree on nothing except that they hated Jesus. Herod and Pilate had no use for each other until Jesus was handed over to them as a prisoner. The Bible says that they then became friends. Even the mob in front of Pilate's palace agreed on one thing—crucify Jesus.

Jesus was "the dreamer" in that society. His message and His actions didn't fit with the establishment. Love, forgiveness, and oneness with the Father set Jesus apart from a society that lived for revenge, domination, and rivalry with God. Jesus' sacrifice on the cross was the ultimate sign of God's love for a world out of sync with Him.

Where do we as a group line up on the continuum of agreement, with the world or with God? Not much has changed since Joseph found himself in a well or since Jesus was nailed to a cross. The world has its ways and God has His. In our stated purpose for existence, whose ways do we follow? When the choice is between mission and money, which wins? Which items on our agenda receive the most attention, people problems or policy problems? How much time at our meetings is devoted to hearing from God or hearing from the world? When and how in our meetings do we actually talk to God in prayer? In the context of our text, how much credence do we give to those who dream the dreams of faith instead of those of practicality?

God was able to use Joseph to further His plan because Joseph was tuned in to God's wavelength. As we continue in our role as God's servants, the distant beat of God's drum will be more apparent to us, and the discordant cacophony of the world will become more distant. As we continue doing God's work, His way, we might hear the world say, "Watch out! Here come those dreamers!"

PRAYER: Dear heavenly Father, we thank You for giving us the dream of eternity and the faith and knowledge of that gift. Strengthen us as You did Joseph to dream Your dreams in a world that is sleepless. Give us the courage and direction to live and act for You in all of our discussions and actions. Hear us, Lord, for Jesus' sake. Amen.

11 GETTING EVEN

Read: Genesis 42:6–17

Although Joseph recognized his brothers, they did not recognize him. Then he remembered his dreams about them and said to them, "You are spies! You have come to see where our land is unprotected."

"No, my lord," they answered. "Your servants have come to buy food." Genesis 42:8–10

The theme of "getting even" is one of the most popular themes that runs through literature. From Captain Ahab, who vows revenge upon the white whale in *Moby Dick*, to Dirty Harry and his famous line "Make my day," getting even reflects a basic human attitude. Whether on the expressway where we are cut off by an erratic driver or at home where we are irritated by a loud neighbor, our motto is: "Don't get mad—get even!"

What a golden opportunity for Joseph, now second in command in Egypt, to get even. There before him—on their knees, no doubt—were his ten brothers. He knew them, but they didn't know him. What scenario would fulfill the desire to get even? How could Joseph repay his brothers for the terror and filth in the empty cistern? What could equal the harsh mistreatment of the Ishmaelites as they hauled him off to Egypt as a slave? What could make up for years spent in an Egyptian prison? These thoughts may have been present in Joseph's mind as he made his decision.

"You are spies!" he shouted. Here came the retaliation. As number-two man, Joseph had the authority to dispense justice as he saw it. Who would dare question him if he were to do away with ten aliens who could possibly be spies? This was Joseph's payback time!

If this group, assembled here for a meeting, knelt before God's chosen, Jesus Christ, what would happen? Not only would He recognize us, He would also understand our inmost thoughts. What could we expect from Him? He could bring up our reluctance to be at this meeting. He could point out examples of sloth, where reports were poorly made (if at all) and assignments were unfulfilled. He could expose our disdain for others in our group, and even for those whom we call leaders. He could also point out how many times our goals were contrary to His. The eternal Judge of all could have us where He wanted us.

But Christ has already exchanged places with us. He has been labeled "The Spy," "The Lazy One," "The Careless One," "The Hate-filled One," even "The Traitor." He has assumed our roles. He has been hauled off as a criminal and executed in our place. This is God's way of getting even! "God made Him who had no sin to be sin for us, so that in Him we might become the righteousness of God" (2 Corinthians 5:21).

As we know, Joseph did not get even, either. He used his position to discover the true attitude of his brothers and eventually to save them and his father. Joseph was truly the son of his heavenly Father, preferring love and forgiveness to punishment.

Be it in finance, property, education, worship, evangelism, community outreach, or other areas, our role as workers in God's kingdom is to mirror God's forgiveness. We are to show God's forgiveness to a world that doesn't deserve to be forgiven. Not only are we to preach to others about God's forgiveness for all, but we are the ones who are in the prime position to demonstrate it.

To be sure, rules need to be followed, policies enforced, and agendas fulfilled, but only after God's forgiveness has been accepted and given to others. That is God's way of getting even. He is holy and He has made it possible for us to be so. He has made us even with Him through Christ.

PRAYER: Dear heavenly Father, we thank You for seeing us as we are and loving us. We thank You for forgiving our sins, corporate and individual, through the shed blood of Christ. Empower us to extend Your forgiveness to those who have sinned against us. Open our hearts and our hands to extend Your love to others. Hear us for Jesus' sake. Amen.

:12: CHURCH AND STATE BOXES

Read: Genesis 47:1–11

Then Joseph brought his father Jacob in and presented him before Pharaoh ... Then Jacob blessed Pharaoh and went out from his presence. Genesis 47:7, 10

The separation of church and state has provoked much discussion. This particular policy is largely unique to the United States. In Europe, the church and the state have been intertwined for centuries. European history is, for the most part, a story of the struggle between the two for supremacy. Today in many European countries the state financially supports the church.

In the United States such a system is unknown. The trend today seems to be leading to even greater separation. Efforts are being made to remove prayer from legislative gatherings, to remove any Christian symbolism from state property, and group prayer has been banned in public schools. Without getting into the pros and cons of this issue, we can say that in the United States church and state have been separated, boxed, and safely sealed from each other. Ours is a compartmentalized system—religion and its practice over here, government and its practice over there.

How strange, then, to read about the meeting between God's great patriarch, Jacob, and a representative of the secular world, the Pharaoh of Egypt. This unique meeting explains the purpose of the events leading up to it. Jacob and his family had come to Egypt in order to escape a famine. Egypt, or the state, became a source of protection and sustenance for God's people, represented by Jacob. Jacob, on the other hand, was there to bless Pharaoh, as stated in the text.

To separate church and state, then, is not only impossible, it is contrary to God's plan. The church needs the state in order to receive protection from disorder and chaos. History shows that the church will survive in times of political unrest, but it operates best in a climate of tranquillity. The state needs the church so that its citizens learn and practice God's way of life here on earth. Jacob and Pharaoh demonstrated this in their meeting.

We have taken the state to task for attempting to isolate itself from the church. But don't we, as the church, do the same thing? How much of our church agenda is actively designed to "bless Pharaoh"? Certainly a part of this blessing comes in the efforts of many Christian churches to carry on community outreach programs: food pantries, child care, counseling services, and recreational facilities. But there is more.

When God gave Abraham the promise of the coming Savior, He used the phrase, "… all people [nations] on earth will be blessed through you [Abraham]" (Genesis 12:3). God was referring to the blessing of the coming Messiah. The Good News of what Jesus did is the greatest blessing we as the church can give the state. Many of our outreach programs will mention the local congregation as the source of the blessing, but will not take the next step and name Jesus Christ as the ultimate Source of good.

What an opportunity we miss when, in our dealings with the state or the community, we leave Jesus at the door. He is the one who told us to give God what God requires and to give Caesar (the government) what he (it) requires. Our government tells us it requires our taxes and allegiance. God tells us that our government also needs the blessing of Christ and His work.

Let us, as a church group, take the lead in blessing our government with our prayers and our support, but also with the presence of Christ in us through word and deed. God is in charge of both church and state, and He wants us to be a blessing to both.

PRAYER: O Lord God, Ruler of all, we ask that as You provide the opportunity, we may work to bless the governments which are Your representatives. Bless with wisdom and compassion those who make laws and enforce them. Give to our elected officials the mind of Christ who came not to be served, but to serve. Empower those who keep the peace to administer their office with justice and with mercy.

Give us the opportunity to speak Your name as the source of all good. Particularly we ask for opportunities to speak of Jesus, our Savior. O Lord, grant these blessings to us and to our government, for Jesus' sake. Amen.

13 GOD'S LARGER PLAN

Read: Genesis 50:15–21

[Joseph said,] "You intended to harm me, but God intended it for good to accomplish what is now being done, the saving of many lives." Genesis 50:20

Most of us like stories with happy endings. Even when it becomes obvious before the ending that "everyone lived happily ever after," we still like a satisfying conclusion, such as the end of Genesis. Structurally, the story of God's beginning plan of salvation is complete in Genesis with the arrival of Jacob and his twelve sons in Egypt. From there the story continues in Exodus with the formation and freeing of Jacob's children. But God in His wisdom provided an important side trip at the end of Genesis—the Joseph story.

We recall the tension and uncertainty of Joseph's unhappy childhood, being sold as a slave and then imprisoned in Egypt for a crime he did not commit. We cheered as God brought him out of prison and into the second highest office in Egypt. We followed with rapt attention as the ten brothers made two visits to Egypt and were treated strangely by the stern ruler. Tension mounted as the brothers pleaded for the life of the youngest brother. At the climax, Joseph revealed that he was their long-lost brother. We watched as they slowly grasped what the consequences of this revelation might be. After Jacob died, the reality finally hit them—now Joseph could get even!

A final meeting followed, with the brothers pleading for forgiveness. Joseph responded with the words of our text, "You intended to harm me, but God intended it for good." Joseph was voicing the theme of God's plan, but God's plan is on a higher plane than the selling of grain to starving people.

God used the terrible sin of human rebellion to show to us how much He loves us. What Satan intended as an assault on God was used by God as a means of embracing us with His love. Joseph was outlining the old story of sin and grace: "You meant harm—God intended good."

The Joseph story is like the story of Jesus Christ. Jesus was hated by His countrymen, sold by His disciple, sentenced to death by the government, died in place of His accusers, and raised to new life as the sign of reconciliation between God and those who sin. The Joseph story is a fitting way to end the first book of the Bible. It is a hand pointing forward through time to God's great salvation.

We are the final chapters in that story. God's grace in Christ has filtered down through the ages and now covers us. Can we as church leaders find ourselves in God's grand picture? Look at the last part of Joseph's speech: ".... to accomplish what *is now being done*, the saving of many lives" (emphasis added). That's where we fit in—saving many lives. This means more than providing education for children, or homes for the homeless, or food for the hungry. As important as these are, the real saving of lives comes with the distribution of the saving Gospel. God has assigned us the role of spreading the Good News of salvation to all.

May our Lord forever fix in our hearts the burning desire to complete His work, to bring the happiest endings to the stories of thousands of people.

PRAYER: Thank You, Lord, for Your far-reaching plan to save all people. Thank You for the example of Joseph, who foreshadowed the salvation of people from eternal damnation through Jesus. We pray that as we have opportunity, we may joyfully tell everyone what You have done in Christ. Amen.

Meetings Through the Year

14 A VOICE CALLING

Read: Isaiah 40:1–8

A voice of one calling: "In the desert prepare the way for the LORD;
make straight in the wilderness a highway for our God."
Isaiah 40:3

One of the universal pet peeves of modern society is the solicitation phone call. Everyone who has a phone gets them. Despite caller ID, answering machines, and cordless phones, these calls still intrude on our peace and quiet. The telephone, once intended as a convenience through which we can reach others, has now become a nuisance through which others can bother us. Apparently solicitation phone calls still work, since companies still hire people to make them.

God's solicitation calls began many years ago, not on the phone, but in the desert. His strangely dressed caller was named John, a man whose task it was to announce the coming of the Messiah and prepare the people of Judah for Him. Isaiah foretold this calling in 40:3, saying, "Make straight in the wilderness a highway for our God."

When John said, "Prepare yourself to meet your God," he was not talking about the pre-Christmas frenzy that we endure each year. Getting ready to meet God does not involve shopping, baking, partying, or decorating. Nor does it involve children's programs, pageants, hanging of the greens, exchanging Christmas cards, candlelight services, or Christmas newsletters. Preparing to meet God is done in the vast wastelands of our hearts. No wonder Isaiah referred to all of this preparation as taking place in the desert.

Our hearts are indeed deserts, places where Christ-like fruit has a hard time growing. The waters of God's forgiveness often evaporate before they can be applied to others. What was once a pathway for God's Word has been blocked by avalanches of monetary, social, and personal concerns. Deep gullies of selfishness, arrogance, and revenge have eroded what was the fertile farmland of spiritual growth. As we hear God's unsolicited call, we look around and see our hearts indeed decimated, ruined, and barren.

Perhaps this Advent season our hearts should be directed not at a Christmas celebration, but at an Advent "clean-out and fix-up." How foolish to work up a frenzy to indulge ourselves for a day in the warm fuzzies of Christmas past, when out in the cold awaits our Lord, wanting to come in and live in our hearts throughout the entire year.

As workers in God's kingdom, should we not sometime during these pre-Christmas days mention to our people the fact that Christ invites us to follow and trust Him? What a massive construction job it would be if God's people would indeed begin building superhighways of love and compassion and bridges of reconciliation, all in preparation for the coming of Jesus!

All of these road projects aren't necessary to receive a plaster image of a baby in a styrofoam manger in a cardboard stable. Nor are they necessary to commemorate the anniversary of the real event 2000 years ago. God already took care of those arrangements. This renovation work is absolutely necessary to receive a returning Lord Jesus, whose last discourses urged us to keep watch for Him. The catch is that we don't know when He'll return. Wouldn't it be interesting if He chose to return while we are recreating His first coming?

Consider this short meditation as the voice crying in the wilderness of our hearts, God's unsolicited solicitation disturbing our peace to offer us life in Him.

PRAYER: Dear Lord Jesus, as we gaze at the chaos that Christmas has become, we ask Your forgiveness for our adding to that chaos through misplaced activities and neglecting to read Your Word and talk to You in prayer. Enable us to lead Your people to see You not just as the Great Gift in a manger, but as their Savior on a cross. Help us all to draw closer to You during this Advent season so that our celebration of Your birth may indeed be a rebirth of devotion in our hearts. This we ask in Your name and for Your glory. Amen.

:15 SEEKING TRUE WISDOM

Read: Matthew 2:1–12

After Jesus was born in Bethlehem in Judea, during the time of King Herod, Magi from the East came to Jerusalem and asked, "Where is the one who has been born King of the Jews? We saw His star in the East and have come to worship Him." Matthew 2:1, 2

We have reached that "blah" time of year. The anticipation and excitement of Christmas is over. Decorations are gone, gifts are either exchanged, broken, or used up. We have returned to what we call normal. To add to the blahs, it's dark when we get up and dark when we return home. In many parts of the country, winter's cold has established itself in earnest. Bright days, warm temperatures, and the first signs of spring are a long way off.

But like a bright point of light comes the story of the Wise Men seeking the newborn King of the Jews. Part of what makes this story so remarkable is the status of these men. From all that can be deduced from the term "Magi," they were each a combination of highly educated scientist and theologian. On the one hand they studied the stars and their movements in great detail; on the other they studied ancient writings of great religions, perhaps to deduce what lay in the future. They were evidently men of some wealth to be able to finance a trip of this magnitude.

Another remarkable part of the story is the star. That star has been the center of so many works of art, songs, stories, and even theological and scientific studies that its wonder may be lost on us. Perhaps this star, in the style that God occasionally uses, was a star that only these trained astronomers would notice. To them it was a magnificent discovery; the average person probably wasn't even aware of it.

This star was seen and tracked by the Wise Men because it spoke their language. God is the master of fitting the language of His Word to those who need to hear it. To the Magi—a star, to shepherds—angels, to you and me—a newborn Child. The message remains the same for all of us—God's tremendous love for human beings. Be it a star, an angel, or a Child, God wants us to know how much He loves us.

Perhaps God's purpose in coming to us in the dark and cold of winter is to shine through our "blahs" and inspire us to move forward. We have more than a star and an obscure prophecy to guide us. We have the accomplished work of Jesus Christ to inspire us and His timeless words to guide us. As the burdens of a new year weigh upon us and the road ahead looks dark and foreboding, God comes to us with the light of the eternal Star and the always-present Word to guide us.

So in the language of this story of the Wise Men, "Let's mount up and move out! The star is out in front and the new King awaits."

PRAYER: Lord God, heavenly King, we thank You at this dark time of year for sending to us the true Star of Bethlehem, Jesus our Savior. Thank You for enabling us to recognize Him among all the false lights of our time. Inspire us to continue the work You have given us to do. Sharpen our minds, unburden our wills, and energize our reluctant hearts so that Your Kingdom may move forward in this place. We ask these things in the name and for the sake of Jesus our Lord. Amen.

1:6 ONE FACE IS ENOUGH

Read: 2 Kings 20:1–11

"Go back and tell Hezekiah, the leader of my people, 'This is what the LORD, the God of your father David, says: I have heard your prayer and seen your tears; I will heal you. On the third day from now you will go up to the temple of the LORD. I will add fifteen years to your life.'" 2 Kings 20:5–6a

The month of January is named for the Roman god, Janus, who is portrayed in pictures with two faces. One face looks backward and one face looks forward, an apt description of the first month of the year. At this time we look backward at what happened in the old year, some good things and some bad, but most things past and over with.

We probably spend more time looking forward to new opportunities, new plans, and new experiences. If only looking forward could reveal what lies ahead. In this reading from 2 Kings, we hear about one of the few individuals who was given an exact timetable for the future. That individual was Hezekiah, a remarkably good king of Judah. In answer to his prayer for healing, God said, "Yes," and then, "I will add fifteen years to your life."

Think about that for a moment. Do we really want to know the exact amount of time we have left? Our lives might turn into a frenzy of activity as we madly dash about squeezing every last experience and accomplishment out of our desires. Or conversely, our lives might shut down, as we sit back and count the days and hours still remaining. In either case, life would be abnormal, and probably unpleasant.

Fortunately, we have a view of the future that is visible only one day at a time. It is much like driving in heavy fog, our headlights only able to reach a few yards ahead. We must therefore exercise extreme caution, reduce our speed, and stay mentally aware of our surroundings.

God wants our lives to run that way. He does not give us a typed schedule of future events in our lives. We do not have a timetable of the approaching year, which programs for us all the good and bad things to come. Since we live in a world pockmarked by sin, bad things will come our way, just as they did last year. We know that not even Janus could solve those problems, he could only look at them.

We don't need Janus. We have what we need—a God who knows all things, a God who not only can see the future, but has promised to guide us through it. This does not mean we will never encounter an upset in the new year. Many potholes are waiting for us on life's road, some of which we will hit directly.

But our God has told us over and over, "I have loved you with an everlasting love" (Jeremiah 31:3), and "I give them [My sheep] eternal life, and they shall never perish; no one can snatch them out of My hand" (John 10:28). St. Paul echoed this same concern as he wrote, "He who did not spare His own Son, but gave Him up for us all—how will He not also, along with Him, graciously give us all things?" (Romans 8:32).

God's will for us, as it was for Hezekiah, is to keep doing His work. Letting God do the driving is infinitely better than doing it ourselves. He can see; we can't. He knows the future; we don't. Therefore we can concentrate on our work, while God does His—and He does it very well.

PRAYER: Dear Lord, we thank You for another year of grace in which You allowed us to work for You. In Your wisdom, You have veiled the future so we can concentrate on the present. Increase our faith in You and Your love for us. Give us the gifts needed to do Your work in this place during the coming year. We thank You for each other and for the time we have together to praise and honor You. In Jesus' name. Amen.

1:7 THE CORPORATE IMAGE

Read: Isaiah 53:1–5

He had no beauty or majesty to attract us to Him, nothing in His appearance that we should desire Him. Isaiah 53:2

The business world is a tough world. Eat or be eaten, grow or die, conquer or be conquered. These succinct expressions are all too familiar to those involved with the give and take of the corporate world. They live with the ever-present motto: "Produce more or use the door!"

This tough business attitude has also invaded the church. Churches today look at one another as business rivals. The community is the market, feeling good is the product, and the annual report is the gauge of success or failure. If income, membership, and public approval are up, business is good. If not, some drastic adjustments in policy, product, and procedure are in order.

Now look at God, who is reporting on His marketing strategy through Isaiah. Tough business tycoons, upon reading this plan, throw up their hands in horror as every rule in the corporate world is broken. The strategy rests on only one employee, coming from nowhere, without a degree in anything. He has no personal charisma, nothing that even comes close to the polished, slick, Madison Avenue image. Furthermore, He is the object of corporate ridicule, as evidenced by the marks of abuse He wears.

Rather than extracting every advantage from clients, this poor wretch takes responsibility for their mistakes and bad deals. He willingly endures one bankruptcy after another. Without any credit, and owing millions in back taxes piled up by others, He is banished from the board room only to be convicted and executed by His competitors.

Such is God's man on Wall Street, or on our street. During these forty days of Lent, we have the opportunity to reacquaint ourselves with God's way of doing business by following the despised and rejected Man who is our business partner. More than a partner, He is our Savior, who ached for the return of the one who betrayed Him, whose look brought back another who had also deserted Him, and who, when nailed to the cross, prayed for those who did it to Him—which includes us!

Even beyond these forty days of intensive training, we, the visible church, are able to conduct business God's way. Our product is not the ability to make others feel good, but the Good News that God wants all to be saved. Our method is not to lure in the customers with temporary treats, but to proclaim God's plan of salvation in word and deed. Our goal is not to gain members, but to make disciples.

The business world is tough, but the spiritual battle for souls is even tougher. Pitted against us is none other than the inventor of evil, Satan himself. No earthly strategy, no five-year plan, no community analysis will ever defeat him. The only victor over Satan and his products of sin and death is Jesus Christ. He proved it in the desert, on the road, in the city, on the cross, and at the grave. Through Him, God gave us all the success we need. Our motto: "God gave more—there's the door—to life!"

PRAYER: Heavenly Father, open our eyes during this season to see things Your way. Bend our wills to follow Yours as we carry on Your work. In Jesus' name. Amen.

:18: WHO IS STAYING WITH YOU?

Read: Luke 24:13–35

As they approached the village to which they were going, Jesus acted as if He were going farther. But they urged Him strongly, "Stay with us, for it is nearly evening; the day is almost over." So He went in to stay with them. Luke 24:28, 29

The joyful exhilaration of Easter is past. The cries of "He is risen!" still ring in our ears. The life-changing news of new life, now and hereafter, makes each day a new adventure in grace. Now it is time to get back to everyday life, time to return to our village of Emmaus.

Such was the prospect of the two disciples who were trudging home after the disturbing events of the weekend. They had heard unfounded reports that Jesus had risen from the dead, so they were confused, dejected, and, in God's plan, ready for a surprise.

How much different are we from these two disciples as we also trudge our way back into post-Easter life? True, we have been told of Jesus' resurrection, experienced the joy of worship, and gathered with friends and family on this special day. But now it's back to everyday life: the job, a new sports season, planning for spring and summer. In the church it's time to conclude the festival portion of the church year, looking ahead to the downside when attendance drops along with contributions. It is indeed a long walk back.

To no one's surprise, we are not alone. Lots of strangers would like to accompany us and perhaps even cheer us up with tales of exciting new plans, programs, and opportunities. As we approach our dwelling, which of these strangers will we invite in to stay with us?

Don't look at faces or dress or demeanor. They all want our attention and business. Among them is one who gives instead of takes. He begins at the beginning, showing our real need for forgiveness and peace with God. He traces the thread of God's grace through the pages of history. He zeroes in on the one who satisfies the demands of the Law and at the same time offers life. He is the one who waits for us to invite Him in. In what disguise does Jesus come to us this year?

It might be husband or wife, son or daughter, employer or employee, stranger or friend, ally or enemy! God delivers His message of hope through many strange messengers. The test is: Whom will you choose to stay with you?

Through the work of the Holy Spirit, the choice is made. Jesus Christ is our constant house guest, sitting at our table, joining in our conversations, adding to our plans. At the meal He prepared, Christ truly makes Himself known to us in the eating and drinking of His body and blood. He wants His life to dwell in ours.

The emotional high of Easter will wear off. The new clothes will get old, and the eggs will eventually turn into egg salad. But Jesus, our Friend and Brother, stays with us and makes each day a new adventure in real living.

PRAYER: Thank You, Lord Jesus, for accompanying us on our post-Easter walk. Be present at our tables, dinner and business, and reveal Yourself to us at Your table as we gather around the Sacrament. In Your name we pray. Amen.

19 NEW POWER FOR OLD MACHINES

Read: Acts 2:1–13

All of them were filled with the Holy Spirit and began to speak in other tongues as the Spirit enabled them. Acts 2:4

At last, most people recycle. We have even dressed up the language of recycling. What used to be "junk" is now "recyclable." "Used" is now known as "pre-owned," and the stuff we grew up with is now "antique." At best, recycling preserves many natural resources; at worst, it makes for another community-interest topic to be championed.

Recycling is not new; God has been doing it for years. God recycles people. He finds them "pre-owned" by Satan—misused and abused by sin, and ready for the eternal trash heap known as hell. By the redeeming power of Jesus Christ, we are recycled in His image. We are equipped with a new life and new power, provided by the Holy Spirit.

Such is the wonder of the Pentecost miracle. The disciples had only recently been salvaged by our Lord's resurrection and given new hope by His ascension. They were gathered, awaiting reassignment, when the Holy Spirit performed a monumental miracle. Hear about it again from Acts 2:4: "All of them were filled with the Holy Spirit and began to speak in other tongues as the Spirit enabled them."

The Holy Spirit's great miracle was not found in the "other tongues" or languages, but in the hearts of the disciples. The great miracle was that these men now spoke about Jesus in public.

Remember the silence when Jesus had asked who men said that He was, as recorded in Matthew 16?

62

Peter finally spoke up for all of them with the correct answer. However, snoring was the only thing heard from them when, in the Garden of Gethsemane, Jesus asked them to keep awake with Him. And where were their voices at Jesus' arrest, save for Peter's desire to defend Him by cutting off Malchus' ear? And their voices were nowhere to be found at His trial, before Pilate, and at the cross. These men had become dumb and eventually absent. Even after Jesus' resurrection, speech came with difficulty. The two Emmaus disciples spoke, but in the wrong direction, as did Thomas, who had to be primed by a personal appearance of Jesus.

The great miracle was that suddenly these once spiritually disadvantaged men were speaking up for all to hear. They were speaking in front of those who just over a month before were condemning their Friend and Savior. They were able to put their hearts into what their mouths were saying. As an added device, the Holy Spirit made their speech understandable to all nations. But the recycled disciples now had voices and they used them.

That same ability is given to us, who are also doing His work. We are most willing to speak up about policies, schedules, plans, criticisms, and suggestions, but when do we get around to speaking about our wonderful Savior and His great work? If, in this meeting, each of us could refer just once to the saving power of Christ, it wouldn't be that hard to speak up about Him in other meetings: home, office, carpool, tennis court, restaurant.

We don't have to even use a strange language; English will do fine.

PRAYER: Heavenly Spirit, come fill us with Your power, Your message, and Your courage. We often are silent when messages need to be given. Open our eyes to the many opportunities we have to speak up for Jesus Christ. Grant to us in this meeting the voices to proclaim His love to each other. Then enable us to continue speaking wherever the Good News needs to be heard. We ask this in the name of Jesus. Amen.

MEETINGS ON FAMILIAR TOPICS

2 OUR FATHER'S BUSINESS

Read: Luke 2:41–50

"Why were you searching for Me?" He asked. "Didn't you know I had to be in My Father's house?" Luke 2:49

One of the most popular unanswered questions about Jesus is: What did He do during His "silent years" (from childhood to the beginning of His public ministry)? We have only one incident recorded from that period and it is from the second chapter of Luke, the same chapter in which His birth is recorded. It is about Jesus as a twelve-year-old on a trip away from home.

At the age of twelve every Jewish boy became a man, a Son of the Law, or "bar mitzvah." At that time he was considered worthy to sit with the men in the synagogue. He was also expected to leave the daily care of his mother and take up the business and lifestyle of his father. Jesus knew who He was, who His true Father was, and that He must take up the business of His Father—not Joseph, but God.

The annual trip to the temple in Jerusalem was just what He needed. Apparently Mary and Joseph looked upon Jesus as a mature, responsible person, for they allowed Him the freedom to travel with the rest of the group on the way home, unconcerned with His where-abouts until a day had passed and they could not find Him.

Frantic with fear after a three-day search, they found Him—at His Father's business! When questioned about it, Jesus' calm, honest response was, "Didn't you know I had to be in My Father's house?" Jesus was reminding

His earthly parents of His true identity and real work. In effect he said, "Since I am now an adult, I must begin My work with My Father—in His place of business."

If only the church today could capture the youthful idealism and excitement of Jesus. We, who have been made sons and daughters of God through Baptism, need to look at our lives from God's perspective. We need to leave the protective and sometimes smothering worldly influence of the earth and take up our Father's business in faith.

Our Father's business brings us together on this occasion. We are not here to save people; all the saving that is needed was done on Calvary. We are not here to promote the self, individual or collective. God has already promoted us to the highest level, calling us sons and daughters. We are here simply to proclaim God's love and forgiveness to those whose lives are in pieces, having been shattered by the Law.

Budgets, schedules, elections, planning, reports, motions, and amendments all can be a part of God's business, but they are not *the* business. *The* business is witnessing to and caring for people and their spiritual needs. That was the business Jesus entered at the age of twelve when He was found in the temple. That's the business we are in as we gather in this place, whatever our age.

Perhaps during this meeting, we should take a few moments of silence to hear again from Jesus, who is indeed present: "Don't you know I must be about My Father's business?" (KJV). These words point us to what we must be about—that is, our Father's business. This should keep us focused.

PRAYER: Dear heavenly Father, thank You for allowing us to work in Your business. We admit that we are unworthy and unable to work for You without Your help. Send Your Holy Spirit to teach us, to inspire us, and to direct us in the ways that are best for Your honor and glory. In Jesus' name. Amen.

2:1 GETTING DOWN TO BASICS

Read: Matthew 28:16–20

Then Jesus came to them and said, "All authority in heaven and on earth has been given to Me. Therefore go and make disciples of all nations." Matthew 28:18, 19a

Whether it is on the fridge door, on the computer screen, in a shirt pocket, or in our heads, everyone has a "to do list." Even at the last earthly meeting of Jesus and His disciples, Jesus produced a "to do list" for them.

Our Lord also has a "to do list," and He is now near the end of it. I can think of no better summary of that list than stanza five of Martin Luther's great hymn "Dear Christians, One and All Rejoice":

He spoke to His beloved Son:
'Tis time to have compassion.
Then go, bright jewel of my crown,
And bring to man salvation;
From sin and sorrow set him free,
Slay bitter death for him that he
May live with Thee forever.' (TLH, 387, v. 5)

At the time of our text, Jesus had only three items left to do: ascend to heaven and rule, evangelize the world, and return to earth to gather believers. Jesus did ascend to heaven and now rules all things, as He said: "All authority in heaven and on earth has been given to Me." When the time is right, Jesus will take care of the last item—returning to take us home. The second one should be of interest to us—evangelize the world, or in His words, "Make disciples of all nations."

Jesus could have accomplished this in a number of

ways. He could have sent His angels. Imagine how many people would attend an evangelism rally lead by angels. Or would you dare to tell an angel, "Not interested!" if he came to your door?

Jesus could have continued His earthly ministry Himself, this time on a global scale. But He didn't. Making disciples, evangelism, mission work—whatever you call it—He left for us to do.

So how are we doing? What are we doing? As we sit here, about ready to conduct business, are we "making disciples"? At this point, all our eyes should gaze downward, hands should wring, and sighs escape as we collectively admit that planning a budget, approving a new worship schedule, or deciding on materials for VBS isn't exactly disciple-making. We in our guilt-laden vision imagine ourselves out ringing doorbells, standing on street corners, hacking our way through jungles, preaching to thousands in order to fulfill Jesus' command.

But Jesus never made specific lists of how we are to obey His command. He merely said, "Make disciples of all nations." Sometimes that means sitting at a well at noontime talking to a lady with a questionable past. Sometimes it means providing an impromptu potluck supper for over 5,000. Sometimes it means attending a wedding and helping a young couple solve a catering problem. Sometimes it means correcting a friend by saying, "Get behind me, Satan!"

So let's lift our eyes, stop the hand-wringing, and get to work solving our disciple-making problems. If what we are doing here contributes to the spreading of the Word, we are working on the correct "to do list." Budgets put dollars to work buying mouths to speak, materials to read, and locations in which to do both. Schedules determine when the Word is shared and who will share it. Deciding on VBS materials is nothing less than deciding how to wrap the precious Gospel as a gift for children.

Evangelizing the world was not accomplished on the Mount of Olives, and it's not accomplished within this meeting room. The disciples left the mount and turned the world upside down. Our real work is not in completing an evening's agenda. Our real work is out there, where our real "to do list" is to be pulled out and used right next to the ones we have on the fridge at home, on the screen, in our pockets, and in our minds.

PRAYER: Dear Savior, thank You for including us in completing Your great "to do list." Keep our faces turned toward the tasks at hand. Open our eyes to the many opportunities to make disciples. Fill us with the same Spirit You have so that Your work is completed before You come to take us home. Amen.

2:2 BRANCHES UNDERGROUND

Read: Romans 11:13–21

You do not support the root, but the root supports you. Romans 11:18

In Paul's definitive treatise on Christian doctrine, otherwise known as the epistle to the Romans, one of the major topics was "What about the Jews?" At the beginning of chapter 11, he asked, "Did God reject His people?" His answer was "By no means!" He then proceeded to show how God preserved, as he called it, "a remnant," a small group that believed in Jesus Christ as their Savior.

Among his arguments was the analogy of farming, particularly the art of grafting branches into rootstock. The procedure is probably most familiar to us in the raising of roses. The hybrid rose stock is grafted into rootstock that is more hearty, thereby producing flowers that are different while nurtured by a plant of maturity and strength. Paul's point of comparison is that the wild Gentile brand of believer has been grafted into the supportive and substantial rootstock of Israel. He warns his Gentile readers not to act as though their life in Christ came about on their own, but to acknowledge that it is a product of God's grace using the roots of the Jewish religion. This practical lesson is worthwhile for us as leaders to ponder.

Being wrapped up in our church jobs, committees, and organizations, we can easily develop tunnel vision, in which we see only our group, our goals, our tasks and, God willing, a successful outcome. We may be aware of a congregation out there who will benefit from what we do. On rare occasions we might consider that what we do will have some effect on people out-side our congregation.

But have we ever looked in the other directions—inward and downward? Returning to Paul's analogy, are we aware that, by God's grace alone, we are one of the branches of God's plant, where Jesus is the main vine? Our very existence as Christians depends upon Him and no one else. Separate us from Christ and we are spiritually dead!

As a part of this marvelous plant, we are also attached to those who have come before us. What a debt of gratitude we owe to God for providing us the stock of our forebears in the faith. They are the ones from years past who established congregations, filled pulpits and classrooms, made evangelism calls, wrote textbooks, and assembled worship materials, doing the work then that we are doing now. They wrestled with problems maybe even greater than ours. They agonized over plans for the future that even now we take for granted. We stand today on the work and accomplish-ments of others.

As we begin our work, let us take a moment to thank God for the hearty stock of God-fearing prede-cessors who built the platform on which we stand. Let us take a longer moment to praise God for the miracle of grace by which we have been grafted into Christ, our True Vine. Then let us look outward to see the areas in which God has given us to grow. What a privilege to be a part of this marvelous creation—the Church!

PRAYER: Dear heavenly Father, we thank and praise You for Your wisdom in establishing Your Church on earth. We thank You for sending heroes of faith who did Your work so well. We praise You especially for pastors, missionaries, teachers, and unsung workers who cleared the way for us to continue today. Keep us in mind of their sacrifices and their gifts so that as You bless our work, we remember theirs. In the name of Jesus. Amen.

2:3: UNLOADING THE LOAD

Read: Exodus 18:13–26

Moses' father-in-law replied, "What you are doing is not good. You and these people who come to you will only wear yourselves out. The work is too heavy for you; you cannot handle it alone."
Exodus 18:17, 18

Burnout was a factor in the lives of God's servants even before the word was invented. Moses had a classic case of burnout.

In Exodus, we read of an incident where Jethro, Moses' father-in-law, stood aghast watching people line up for a day-long wait to consult with Moses. Jethro told Moses, "The work is too heavy for you; you cannot handle it alone." He therefore suggested that Moses choose some qualified men to assist in dealing with the smaller problems while Moses concentrated on the larger ones.

Another sign that Moses was wearing down, even after helpers were chosen, is found in Numbers 20, where Israel was once again complaining about a lack of water. God clearly instructed Moses to speak to a rock and water would come out. Note Moses' frustration level as he confronted the people with this: "Listen, you rebels, must we bring you water out of this rock?" (Numbers 20:10). Moses reverted to name-calling and then announced that he and Aaron would bring the water—not even mentioning God.

As the final proof that not all was right, Moses hit the rock three times instead of speaking to it as God had clearly directed. God in His mercy sent water for His people, but later confronted Moses for his unfaithfulness.

Burnout happens to the best of us—too many decisions, demands, and frustrations, and not enough time. Frustrations rise like an evil tide, threatening to overwhelm us. At times like these, we need to listen, not to fathers-in-law, shrinks, or even to our own egos, but to the one whom God has sent to be our "load-bearer." Peter wrote, "Cast all your anxiety on Him because He cares for you" (1 Peter 5:7).

Christ "did not come to be served, but to serve, and to give His life" (Mark 10:45) because Jesus is the true load-bearer who "took up our infirmities and carried our sorrows" (Isaiah 53:4). If Christ's back was broad enough to carry our sins, He is surely capable of shouldering our frustrations. The writer of Hebrews reminds us, "We do not have a high priest [Jesus] who is unable to sympathize with our weaknesses, but we have one who has been tempted in every way, just as we are—yet was without sin" (Hebrews 4:15).

Jethro's warning to Moses is also a warning to us, "The work is too heavy for you; you cannot handle it alone." But unlike Jethro, who advised Moses to select qualified help, God has already supplied us with a qualified helper—Jesus Christ, His Son.

Prayer is the device for unloading all the worry and grief we carry. Forgetting proper church language and well-turned phrases, we can cry out to our Savior, "Enough already! I need help, Lord, and You are the only one who can give it to me. Please carry my load for me while I follow where You lead."

PRAYER: O Lord, help our unbelief to change to a firm grasp on Your promises. We are weak; You are strong. Help us to let go of our burdens so You may bear them for us. According to Your holy will, direct us to levels of success that are beneficial for Your kingdom and our growth in grace. Hear us, Lord, for Jesus' sake. Amen.

2:4 NUMBERING OUR DAYS

Read: Psalm 90

Teach us to number our days aright, that we may gain a heart of wisdom. Psalm 90:12

I recall from childhood a line from the collect offered on behalf of those whose loved ones had died. It said, "Teach us to number our days that we may apply our hearts unto wisdom and finally be saved." In childlike fashion, I was fascinated by the phrase "number our days." Being at the beginning of the educational highway, numbers were a big part of school. What was meant by that phrase? Were we to sit down and write a number on each day, just like on the calendar? Were we supposed to add them up like we added numbers in school?

As I grew older and wiser, I came to understand the phrase "number our days" as "keep track of what you do with your time" or "make the maximum use of the time God gives you." Yet the childlike interpretation might not be that far off.

What would happen if we wrote a number on each day of our life? I don't mean the number from the calendar. Rather, each day would have its own number, just like the Bible says "number our days." Day #1 we would not remember, of course; our parents would remember that one for us. The same goes for Day #26, our Baptism Day. That one, of even more importance, would be remembered into eternity.

Then follows the unbroken succession of numbered days: #2,372, the first day of school; #6,843, graduation from high school; #9,782, wedding day; #10,329, birth of first child, and so the parade continues. Each day a new float passes by with its display of good and bad. For some the parade is short; for others it is quite long. But be assured the last float will come at some time, with its ominous label—"the End."

"The End" is why the adult interpretation is needed. If each day has a number, we need to make each day important. We need to make each day amount to something.

By our count, our Lord Jesus' last day before His resurrection was #12,160. That is not very many days, when you consider that He used only 1,095 of them in His public ministry. But Jesus made every day count, because in His 1,095 days He accomplished all the work His Father gave Him to do. How significant that at 3 P.M. on day #12,160, He was able to say, "It is finished!"

Each of us has a different numbered day. How significant that day becomes as each of us brings his or her personal numbered day together. They all become one, a day in which to accomplish something for the Lord.

Our individually numbered days belong to God, not us. He alone gave them to us and He alone knows how many we each have. Therefore, our duty and privilege is to use each day wisely, to maximize each day's potential. The time we contribute to this meeting needs to be the best we can give.

Before we speak, before we ask a question, before we make a motion, we need to make sure that what we do is truly numbering our day "aright" by measuring each day against the love that God filled it with. We can say it no better than did Moses in Psalm 90:17:

> May the favor of the Lord our God rest upon us;
> establish the work of our hands for us—
> yes, establish the work of our hands.

PRAYER: Eternal Father, we thank You for giving each of us our measure of time to use in Your service. As we meet to accomplish something for You, help us to filter out all that would waste time. Fill us with the urgency of Christ, who in His short time accomplished all that You gave Him to do. If it is Your will, bring to completion all that we plan so Your kingdom may grow. We ask all this in Jesus' name. Amen.

2:5 MAKING CHOICES

Read: Acts 1:12–26

Then they prayed, "Lord, You know everyone's heart. Show us which of these two You have chosen to take over this apostolic ministry, which Judas left to go where he belongs." Acts 1:24, 25

We may have heard about drawing straws, throwing dice, tossing a bat, heads down–hands up, secret ballot, and Roberts' Rules of Order. People can be very creative when it comes to making decisions. The matter of election is in addition to the mere mechanics of voting, drawing straws, or motioning. Our national process of politics is built on selling an idea or a person. When entering an election, one needs to be prepared for giving and taking, buying and selling, pay-ups and pay-backs. It can be a dirty business.

Yet the Lord, in managing His business, allows us to make choices. We choose leaders, budgets, five-year plans, contractors, and paint color. What would life in God's Kingdom be like if all choices and policies were already made? Who among us would want the responsibility of hauling around a one-ton manual with 1.5 million pages, much less the task of reading it to find which policy fits our particular need? God has a better plan. He lets us choose.

When choosing Matthias as the replacement for Judas, the disciples first looked into God's policy manual, Scripture. To their satisfaction, they found a precedent for completing the number of the Twelve. Whether we agree with their exegetical conclusion is beside the point. The point is that they began by checking with the Chairman of the Board. Perhaps many of the issues that confront us today do have a precedent in the Bible. After all, much of the Bible is about people like us. What did they do? Did God approve or disapprove?

The second thing the disciples did was pray. Their prayer was not a tightly drawn contract that would squeeze a predetermined "Okay" from God. They relinquished the matter into God's hands. They began by reminding God and themselves that only He knew their hearts. He alone could bring to the outside what already existed inside. Then they merely asked for God to show them which of the two He had already chosen. That is faith; that is wisdom; that is how to do an election.

We know God will make the correct choice because He always has. He chose His Son as our only hope of salvation. He chose us to be recipients of that salvation. Now He allows us to tap into His immeasurable resources to make more choices.

As the meetings go on and as the votes are taken, would it not be a good idea to stop between "Is there any more discussion?" and "I call the question," to say, "Lord, show us what You want done"?

PRAYER: Dear heavenly Father, give us the faith necessary to put our agenda in Your hands. Move us to look to You for guidance in choosing people, activities, and projects. Open our eyes and ears to be sensitive to the real needs of Your people. Put into us the mind of Christ who humbly bowed to Your plan and went to the cross for us. Hear us, Lord, for the sake of Your first choice for us. Amen.

2:6 GOD'S RULES OF ORDER

Read: 1 Corinthians 14:26–33

For God is not a God of disorder but of peace. 1 Corinthians 14:33

The gospels do not record the phrase, "... and Jesus laughed." They do record, however, that He wept.

As in any well-written story, the events that are unusual get into print; those that are commonplace are not recorded because they are the rule. How could Jesus have attended parties and not laughed? How could He hold and bless children and not laugh and be amused at their antics? Indeed it is recorded that after the disciples' first trial run at ministry (Luke 10:21), Jesus rejoiced. In the Old Testament, the Lord laughs at the attempts of His enemies to win.

Perhaps in this vein, the Lord looks upon those who, with test tube, volt meter, and litmus paper, solemnly announce that the universe came into being by itself, through chance. To prove their findings they hold up their "tools" as the evidence. How God must laugh at such silliness. He, who brought forth the universe merely by His word, "has them in derision."

What has fooled science into supporting evolution is the meaning of our text, "God is not a God of disorder but of peace." What else would you expect of a God of order than to find species which resemble each other, but in ascending degrees of complexity? What else would come from God but a perfectly balanced earth with just the right amount of oxygen, just the right distance from the sun, and just the correct tilt to its axis? What we recognize as the trademarks of an order-loving God, science sees as gigantic rolls of the dice, coming up with double sixes each time.

God's perfect order was flawed in only one area—ours. We and our parents destroyed God's order and peace with our willful disobedience, and we are still at it. God's sense of order and peace put the words into the announcement of the angels to the shepherds of Bethlehem, "On earth peace to men on whom His favor rests" (Luke 2:14). In the language of today they would say, "Enough already! Let's have peace between God and people. No more disorder!" God brought peace when He sent His Son among us, who truly gave us the sign of peace, the cross.

Now we, who profess to live that way, are gathered here to carry on God's campaign of peace. May peace prevail in this meeting. Let disorder and the statement "Me first!" be banished from the room. Let all things be done in order. We who wear the cross in our hearts and minds can do no other.

Perhaps, as peace prevails in this meeting, God's smile will warm us all and bring forth smiles on our faces also.

PRAYER: God, we Your servants are gathered here to do Your work. Help us to do it as You do, with order and peace. Keep from us the selfishness that marred the peace in our first home, paradise. Give us the joy and confidence of Christ, who rules all things for the benefit of His church. According to Your will, grant success to the plans we make and the actions we take so Your kingdom will be extended. We ask this as Your children through Christ our Lord. Amen.

2:7 THE VOICES OF DISSENT

Read: Numbers 16:1–35

They came as a group to oppose Moses and Aaron and said to them, "You have gone too far! The whole community is holy, everyone of them, and the LORD is with them. Why then do you set yourselves above the LORD's assembly?" Numbers 16:3

Many meetings are unpleasant, having a disagreement, a difference of opinion, or in the case of this text, a rebellion as the main agenda item. Ever since the emergency meeting in Eden between God, Adam and Eve, and Satan, there have been meetings ranging from mild disagreements to out-and-out rebellion. One does not need to list all of the topics that have led to these unpleasantries. Each person here has his or her own list and the memories to go with them.

At the bottom of most of these conflicts is the line from this text, mouthed by Korah and his followers, "You have gone too far!" In words of today he would say, "I've had it up to here and I'm not going to take it anymore!" What is it that he has "had up to here"? Again in his words, "Why ... do you set yourself above the LORD's assembly?" We have heard that phrase before. Perhaps we have even used it.

From children who chafe under the domination of older brothers and sisters to employees who feel exploited by unfeeling management, everyone has been in Korah's position. The church is no different. "The pastor runs everything." "It's the same ones who decide everything." "Just because they've got the money, they think they can run the show." People have a problem with being treated in a manner that doesn't fit their self-image.

From where does this universal complaint come? Its ugly head first appeared in the Garden of Eden, where the old serpent, Satan, came with this same theme, "Be more than you are!" Somewhere in Satan's former angelic state he desired more status and was promptly ushered out of heaven. He now reflected that prideful urge in his challenge to Eve. His tune did not change, even when confronting Christ in the wilderness of temptation. Satan said that if Jesus was God's Son, He could be fed by making stones into bread, He would be protected if He jumped down from the temple heights, and that all the world would be His if He would worship Satan. Satan's appeal is to make people feel bigger than they really are. Fortunately Jesus banished Satan, using the eternal Word as His weapon.

This brings us to meetings of warring egos. Many times the real issue is which ego will win. When these confrontations occur in the church, the egos are still there but oftentimes covered over with an issue of church business or policy. Korah wanted more say in running the show. James and John, at the prompting of their mother, wanted more status. The disciples' favorite topic at times was who was the greatest.

It is time to look around and see the landscape. All of us are carrying the same load of sin and wearing the same smelly uniform of inherited guilt. As Paul says, "There is no difference, for all have sinned and fall short of the glory of God" (Romans 3:22–23). Under the cross of Christ we are all dwarfs, misshapen and ugly. How can we pretend we are able to see over the heads of others?

Compared to God, we are nothing. Justified by God, we are everything, and all equal. When this is our view—all saved by God's grace—then we are able to discuss the issues, not personalities. Jesus took care of the ego problem on the cross. He now allows us to tackle the Kingdom problems in meetings.

May our gracious Lord help us to bring His Spirit of reconciliation to the table. May all egos and firearms be checked at the door. May the Lord turn an unpleasant beginning into a glorious ending, just as He has done for us in Christ.

PRAYER: Merciful Father, we confess to You that our over-inflated selves have often gotten in the way of Your work. For Jesus' sake, forgive us these sins of pride and loveless-ness.

Fill us instead with the Spirit of Your Son, who humbled Himself to fit on the cross in our place. Work in us the mir-acle of reconciliation, that we may embrace each other with both arms. We ask this in the name of Him who holds us in His eternal love. Amen.

2:8 THE OBNOXIOUS PERSONALITY

Read: Luke 14:7–11

When He noticed how the guests picked the places of honor at the table … . Luke 14:7

We can only imagine the scene, since today we are usually a little more subtle in "tooting our own horn." But in Jesus' day there was apparently a pecking order demonstrated by where guests sat at banquets. Imagine, if you can, the elbowing, shoving, and downright nasty remarks made as incipient hopefuls vied for the places of honor.

What followed Jesus' observation of this social warfare is a not-so-subtle parable on humility. But our attention in this devotion is centered on the cause of it all—the obnoxious, pushy personality that tries to dominate meetings, whether social or business. It has something to say on every topic; it doesn't even pretend to hear another point of view; it tries to gather to itself other like-minded personalities. For many meeker souls, it is a cross that must be carried and endured.

A number of thoughts immediately bubble to the top of the "what-to-do-about-it?" agenda. Among them, no doubt, are banishment, impeachment, duct tape, resignation, imprisonment, and the like. One thought rarely even considered is that beneath the obnoxious personality is a person of worth. Buried within the pompousness and the "know-it-all" attitude lies a person with good ideas and Spirit-filled motivation. The package in which they are wrapped is what gives us a headache.

God also has to deal with obnoxious personalities—ours. As St. Paul writes in Romans 3:10ff:

There is no one righteous, not even one;
... All have turned away, they have together become worthless;
... Their throats are open graves; their tongues practice deceit.
The poison of vipers is on their lips.
Their mouths are full of cursing and bitterness.

God loved us, as obnoxious as we are. He paid for each of those obnoxious sins. He sent His Spirit to do the renovation job. Everyone gathered here is a work-in-progress. Some personalities are further along in development than others, but all are being worked on as long as Word and Sacrament are being applied.

We are incapable of repairing an obnoxious personality. Only God can do that, so we leave that work to the master re-shaper of personalities. Jesus ends His parable with the final solution: "For everyone who exalts himself will be humbled, and he who humbles himself will be exalted" (Luke 14:11).

That's how God handles the obnoxious personality, and we can't do any better than He does.

PRAYER: O Merciful and loving Father, as we gather together, we pray that Your Holy Spirit will take over our lives and our personalities. Motivate us to see each other as You do, with eyes of love and forgiveness. At the same time fill us with the desire to subjugate our wills to what is best for Your kingdom. According to Your will, perform the miracle of healing on all of our hurting and damaged personalities. We ask this in Jesus' name. Amen.

2:9 AND NOW ... ABOUT THE COLLECTION

Read: 1 Corinthians 16:1–4

On the first day of every week, each one of you should set aside
a sum of money in keeping with his income, saving it up,
so that when I come no collections will have to be made.
1 Corinthians 16:2

There ... we heard it, the "M-word"—money! We all know the phrase that automatically comes forth from irritated hearers, "All the church is interested in is money!" That phrase is followed by any number of exit speeches, as church members, fringe and otherwise, head for the door.

What is it about money that causes us to become so sensitive? One of the most anticipated days of the year in my home congregation was the day that the report containing the annual contributions came out. At first, people's names were used in the report, but quickly the names were changed to numbers so that what people gave was a secret.

Exact salary figures are closely guarded secrets. Most of us don't even like to tell what we paid for cars, vacations, and houses. On the other hand, we like to know about others' salaries, prices of purchases, and assets. Money certainly has a strange hold on us.

St. Paul handles the subject of the church and money in an interesting way. He wanted the Corinthian Christians to monetarily help out their Christian brothers and sisters in Jerusalem.

First, Paul did not apologize for bringing up the subject. He went directly from discussing the resurrection in chapter 15 to discussing the collection in chapter 16. Giving was a natural and expected part of the new life in Christ, so why apologize for it?

Second, Paul treated money like a servant, not a master. He did not want the collection to occupy center stage, having the more important work of preaching, teaching, praying, and helping muscled out of the way. Nevertheless, giving was to be a big deal, a weekly habit like public worship, the weekly paycheck, and the weekly grocery trip.

But notice that the "collection" was to be made "on the first day of every week," before any of the weekly bills were paid, before there arose unexpected expenses, and before sudden bargains became available. Why? Because that "collection" was really for God— and God comes first.

Squirreled away in that manner, the "collection" was off limits to the giver. It belonged to God and His kingdom. Each giver was putting God first, from the heart, and expressed through the wallet. Paul was actually attacking that strongest of muscles, the one attached from our hearts to our purses. He was saying, "Loosen up! Your heart *and your wallet both belong to God.*"

Third, Paul puts giving into the proper mode, answering the anticipated question, "How much?" "You give," he says, "as God has given to you." How simple! If God allows us large incomes, then He expects a large gift; small incomes merit a small gift. Our gifts are but miniature reproductions of what God has given to us.

Even though church members cringe when the subject of the collection is brought up, church leaders seem to spend much time in their meetings, not on how to give money away, but rather on how to raise it and then how to spend it (or not spend it, as the case may be). Money may seem to be the god from whom blessings flow. Money is important, but only as a servant who pays the bills. It is certainly not a god who dictates policy. God's kingdom is not built on money, it is built on Jesus Christ. Christian congregations owe their allegiance to Christ, not to the local bank or mortgage company. It is Christ who gave His life for us, and He will also give us all the things we need.

When the subject of money comes up, and it certainly will and should, treat it as the servant it is. The love of Christ will rule in your hearts and money will be its messenger service.

PRAYER: Dear Father, we thank You for the contributions Your Spirit has motivated our members to bring. We pray that as good stewards of Your treasury, we may with foresight and prudence use those gifts as You would. Keep us open to the many opportunities You provide for using those gifts to Your glory. As You see fit, give us the monetary resources to do Your work, but not enough to find no need to trust You. Hear us, Lord, for Jesus' sake. Amen.

30 WHERE IN THE BODY ARE WE?

Read: Romans 12:3–8

In Christ we who are many form one body, and each member belongs to all the others. Romans 12:5

E pluribus unum—"out of many are one." So states the inscription on our coins and some government documents. *E pluribus unum* is an apt description of what our founding fathers envisioned for the United States. Unity, however, is not the exclusive goal of this country. Today, many organizations strive for unity in purpose, in personnel, in procedure, and in product. Unity is a hot topic.

In the church, unity has long been a coveted quality. Think of how many "ones" we take for granted in our beliefs and practices: one God, three Persons; one holy, apostolic church; one Lord, one faith, one baptism; even unified budgets. Getting into more practical examples, every pastor's goal is to have a unified congregation, all pulling in the same direction. Many older church-goers recall how wonderful it was when the church worshiped in a unified way, all using the same hymnal and order of worship. Unity is everyone's goal, but how can it be achieved?

St. Paul revealed his rather simple formula in Romans 12:5, "We who are many form one body, and each member belongs to all the others."

How simple! We have no problem recognizing that the church has the "many," meaning many different people with many different talents, ideas, and backgrounds. But Paul wrote, "[they] form one body, and each member belongs to all the others." Can you imagine what would happen if we all believed and practiced *belonging* to each other? We would willingly go along with what our fellow member wanted because "we belong" to him or her. He or she, in turn, would go along willingly with what we want because they "belong" to us. Instead of pulling apart in disunity, we would implode on each other as each of us would struggle to go along with the other. Hardly a picture of unity!

Yet, in many churches, that is the problem. Everyone wants to do the right thing; everyone wants to please the others. The result is that they fall all over each other trying to be "unified." Then what is the problem?

The problem is that in quoting St. Paul in Romans we left out the critical element of unity—Jesus Christ! Paul wrote, "*In Christ* we who are many form one body, and each member belongs to all the others." Trying to achieve unity without Jesus Christ as the Unifier is as impossible as holding up an umbrella without a handle, spraying water without a nozzle, or painting a wall without a roller or brush. Jesus gives us direction, focus, and cohesiveness.

With Jesus as our Unifier, we understand that we are all equal under grace. We understand that our individual lives are now copies of His. We understand that our goal is His goal—to make disciples of all nations. We belong to Him and consequently to each other.

With this true unity as our foundation, let there be differences in background, talent, wealth, and personality. In the hand of Christ all those differences branch out and blossom in true beauty, as does a bouquet of garden flowers. *E pluribus unum*? Absolutely, as long as Jesus is the *unum* and we are the *pluribus*. So our motto reads "out of one are many."

PRAYER: Dear Lord Jesus, we humbly ask that at this time You give us Your grace and mercy, Your vision and insight, Your love and compassion. Make us truly one in You. Amen.

3:1 THE LAST CLASS

Read: Acts 1:6–9

So when they met together, they asked Him, "Lord, are You at this time going to restore the kingdom to Israel?" Acts 1:6

Two weeks of intensive study have been invested. The instructor has put together an impressive array of examples, outside readings, audiovisuals, computer printouts, and interesting, fast-paced class meetings. It is now time for review.

The first question: "What has been the central focus of this unit?" An awkward, agonizingly long silence follows. "Anybody?" pleads the instructor.

Rising in the teacher's mind is a flood of frustration: "Two weeks of work—wasted! Two months of preparation down the drain! What is in these students' heads?!"

Could this have been the reaction of Jesus to the question quoted above? In this case the disciples had received three years of intensive instruction by the Master Teacher Himself. With the pain of the cross behind Him, the glory of the resurrection in full bloom, and His imminent departure at hand, the granddaddy of stupid questions emerged: "Lord, are You going to be the real Messiah and restore David's kingdom now?"

Three years of work down the drain! Didn't these disciples learn anything? Did Jesus have to start over on page one?

Only our Savior could recover without so much as a wince. "It is not for you to know the times or dates the Father has set by His own authority ... ," He replied

(Acts 1:7). In other words, "This is none of your business!" Then Jesus slid beautifully into a statement of what their business was.

At this meeting, where results are to be noted, closure made, and perhaps good-byes said, are there any leftover stupid questions to be asked? "What have we been doing for all this time?" "Is any of this really of any importance?" "Couldn't one person have done this?" "How come nobody appreciates what we have done?" "Why did so-and-so have to be chairman?"

Stupid questions and equally stupid answers often mar last meetings. But stupid as they might be, the presence of our real leader, Jesus Christ, keeps us together and on track. Through His Spirit, He gently reminds us that our work has not been for us, but for Him. Our time spent was not for pay, but for sharing His presence with others. The troubles, disappointments, and hurts of our time together have driven us closer to Him and to each other. In the words of a long-forgotten poet:

Only one life, will soon be past;
Only what's done for Christ will last.

What He did for us has lasted through the time this group has been together and will last into eternity. This may be the last meeting for a while, but not forever. Class will be continued in eternity!

PRAYER: Dear Lord Jesus, we thank You for Your presence and help during our time together. We ask Your forgiveness for the many times we have questioned Your promises and forgotten Your presence. Assist us now to lay aside long-harbored bruises, bent feelings, and frustrated ambitions. Reveal to us the glory and honor of laboring in Your vineyard. Be with each of us as we separate physically. Strengthen the bond of unity that exists with You. We ask these blessings in Your name. Amen.

PRAYERS

FOR THE OPENING OF A MEETING

Our gracious Lord and Master, as we gather here to do the work of Your kingdom, we acknowledge that we are unworthy and unqualified to do so. We bring our separate and collective sins with us, asking You to forgive us for Jesus' sake. Restore to us the joy and anticipation of working in Your kingdom and for Your glory.

Bless our efforts in organizing information, making decisions, and carrying them out. Give us harmony and cohesiveness in our dealings with each other. Above all, grant that what we say and do here may give You glory and serve to further Your kingdom. All this we ask in the name of Jesus. Amen.

Blessed Lord, we thank You for allowing us to gather in this place to carry on Your work. We acknowledge our inability to do any good without Your guidance. Therefore, send Your Holy Spirit among us to open our eyes to see things Your way. Bend our wills to head in the direction You choose. Keep from us the spirit of self-serving and petty meanness that is a trademark of Satan. According to Your will, give us the successes we need to go forward. At the same time, give us enough obstacles to cause us to cling more tightly to Your promises.

Bless our time together and make it produce the fruits of faith that You have ordained. We say all of this by Your command and because of the promise of Jesus, our Savior, to hear us. Amen.

Dear Father in heaven, in Your glorious home the holy angels do Your every bidding and they do it perfectly. We therefore ask, since we are about the same business, that you enable us to do Your work as the angels do. Help us overcome every hindrance that Satan would place in our midst. Keep from us the temptations to do things his way. Rather, free us by Your Holy Spirit to be truly focused on matters of the kingdom.

Bless all who labor for You, both in this place and scattered throughout the world. Give to those who speak for You the power and eloquence necessary to spread Your Word. Give those who labor for You the strength of spirit and body to accomplish Your agenda. Hear us, O Lord, for Jesus' sake. Amen.

Dear Lord Jesus, we thank You for including us among those especially chosen to carry on Your work. Thank You for calling us by the Gospel, making us Your brothers and sisters through Baptism, and sustaining us through Word and Sacrament.

Often we become lost and discouraged in the maze of complexities before us. As our Good Shepherd, lead us through those times of trouble, strengthen our feeble wills, and guide our walk so that we are truly in Your footsteps. Show us the many joyful opportunities we have to help extend and strengthen Your kingdom here and elsewhere.

Bless our pastor(s) and other called workers to perform their duties in accordance with Your will. Make us all one in our determination to serve You well. We pray these things according to Your will and promise in Christ our Lord. Amen.

IN TIMES WHEN HARMONY IS NEEDED

Gracious Lord, heavenly Father, we come to You with heavy hearts, knowing that we are not united in purpose or in procedure. We admit to our individual willfulness, which hinders true unity. Forgive us for such a narrow-minded view of Your work. Fill us instead with the desire to put aside our personal agendas and follow only You. Remove from each of our hearts the desire for selfish goals, and fill us with the joy of doing things You want in the way You would do them. Instruct us as we need instruction. Correct us as we need correction. Bring us together in this meeting so Your work might continue in this place. Hear us, Lord, for the sake of Jesus, Your Son, our Lord. Amen.

BEFORE A VOTE

O blessed Lord, who constantly guides and directs the affairs of Your Church, we pray that now Your will might be done through us in this voting procedure. Help each of us to see clearly what the choices are, what the possibilities for Your kingdom are, and how we can serve You in the best way.

Thank You for allowing us this privilege of making choices in Your service. Help us all, after the choice is made, to work to fulfill the obligations of our vote. Make us strong in faith and dedication that, with this decision made, we may move forward for You. In Jesus' name. Amen.

BEFORE A DIVINE CALL IS MADE

O Lord Jesus, at this important point in our history, come among us with Your Holy Spirit to guide and direct us in our voting. We thank You for allowing us this privilege of choosing the one who is to serve in this place.

Remove mundane, earthly concerns from our thinking, and fill us instead with the wider vision of the needs of Your kingdom. Help us to achieve unity of purpose in choosing the one who will serve You best.

We thank You for all the dedicated men and women who serve You so faithfully. Direct our voting so that the one we choose may also be numbered among those who carry Your name with distinction. Make us, therefore, extensions of Your will and grace. Hear us, Lord, as You have so promised. Amen.

TO BREAK AN IMPASSE

Dear heavenly Father, we come at this point in our meeting to a time when we can go no further. Whether from sinful desires or misguided zeal, we cannot decide what to do. We therefore come to You for help and guidance. Remove from us what is hindering Your work. Change minds and hearts to be in accordance with Your will. Create in us a willingness to go the extra mile when it is necessary. As You have so many times before, work the miracle of reconciliation among us and give us a clear path of action. Hear us, O Lord, as You have promised to do for Jesus' sake. Amen.

FOR NEW MEMBERS

Blessed Lord, we thank You for bringing to us these souls who need the care and concern of this gathering. We thank You for bringing them to faith in our dear Savior, for sustaining them in that faith, and for allowing us to minister to their needs.

Help us to help them in their Christian walk, nurturing them through Your Word, strengthening them through the sacraments, and building them up through the fellowship of the saints. Make them a blessing to this congregation as they live and serve among us. Keep us all safe under the protection of Your mighty arm. We say all of this according to Your command and promise, in Jesus' name. Amen.

FOR MEMBERS WHO HAVE LEFT

Dear heavenly Father, we come before You with heavy hearts. We grieve on behalf of these, Your children, who are leaving the circle of this group. You, alone, O Lord, know the movements of hearts and desires. You, alone, O Lord, dictate the course of events. We therefore praise and thank You for how You administer Your kingdom and Your distribution of its members.

We thank You for our having had the privilege of ministering to the needs of these souls. We now pray that according to Your will they be protected from evil and from the assaults of the Evil One. Keep them close to You as You have in the past. Move them to seek You each day in prayer and devotion. Bring us all to that glorious day when we can be united once more with each other and with You.

In Jesus' name. Amen.

FOR HELP IN TIMES OF FINANCIAL TROUBLE

Dear Father in heaven, all of our wants are truly known to You. Therefore we come before Your throne humbly asking Your help as we struggle to meet our financial obligations. We remember how Jesus our Savior told us that in putting Your kingdom first, all the other things would be taken care of. O Lord, we do seek to extend and build up Your kingdom, therefore we ask that You supply us with the financial help needed to do Your work. According to Your will, help us find a way for this to be accomplished.

Also, Lord, keep us humble and trusting in You only as the source of our help. Keep from us the desire for greater finances, lest we stop trusting You and instead make money our god. Hear us, O heavenly Father, for Jesus' sake. Amen.

FOR NEW OFFICERS AND LEADERS

O Lord, we humbly thank You for providing us with leaders to carry on Your work among us. We praise Your name for leading these people to assume the many duties that are a part of this congregation's work. Send Your Holy Spirit upon them and fill them with renewed eagerness to begin work for You. Give them strength and health to be able to carry on their many duties. Provide them with daily guidance and encouragement from Your Word. When the days are long and the burdens of office heavy, sustain them, Lord, with Your tender care.

Grant that we, as fellow workers, may support them with our prayers and our cooperation in the days to come. Give us all the joy of working together for You. When our work is done, gather us to Yourself in the eternal joys of heaven. These things we pray in the name of Jesus, our Lord and Savior. Amen.

FOR HELP IN TIMES OF TROUBLE

Heavenly Father, we know that You look with mercy upon Your children. We therefore humbly ask that You rescue us from this time of trial. Keep Satan from gaining an advantage from this trouble, and turn it instead into a victory for Your truth and justice.

Keep us united in our purpose of serving You and let not bickering and fighting divide us. Give each of us the strength and determination to continue the struggle. Bring us forth from this trial more unified and more certain of our role in Your kingdom.

Hear us, Lord God, for the sake of Your glory and through the merits of Your Son, our Lord Jesus Christ. Amen.

PRAYERS OF THANKSGIVING

FOR THE RESOLUTION OF A PROBLEM

Our heavenly Father, source of all good, we give You thanks and praise that in this time of trial You have graciously answered our prayers and brought us safely to a pleasing solution. We thank You for giving to us this opportunity to grow in our faith and trust in Your promises. Help us now to move forward in faith, knowing that You are at our side. According to Your will, give success to the plans we make and to the efforts we give for Your sake. We give our thanks and praise to You in the name of Christ, our Lord. Amen.

FOR AGREEMENT IN CALLING A WORKER

Dear Lord, at this time we heartily give You thanks for moving among us and choosing a person to carry on Your work in this place. All glory to You, O Lord, for Your wisdom and insight into our real needs and for Your understanding of our role in Your plan.

Give to our candidate the blessing of Your divine counsel. Make _____ conscious of Your presence and Your will so that Your kingdom may prosper. Give us the patience needed to help our candidate, the persistence in prayer to sustain _____, and the power of faith to trust You for the correct outcome.

All this we pray in the name of Jesus, our Savior. Amen.

FOR REACHING A GOAL

Merciful Lord, we give You heartfelt thanks for answering our prayers and allowing us to reach our goal. You alone, O Lord, know what unseen obstacles were in the way. By Your mercy You have removed them and allowed us to complete our work. For this we praise and thank You.

Help us to continue, using the blessings of Your grace to move forward, strengthening Your people in faith and extending the borders of Your kingdom. Keep us humble in success, that Satan may not use this blessing to his advantage. Make us continually aware of the needs of Your people whom we serve.

Praise and glory be Yours for Your wisdom and guidance through our days together. These thoughts of our hearts we bring to You because of the invitation of Jesus, our Lord. Amen.

FOR MONETARY STABILITY

Our heavenly Father, we praise and thank You for Your grace in allowing us to continue Your work without financial worry. Our financial needs have been met solely through Your providence. We also thank You for moving the hearts of Your people to give from their hearts for the work of Your kingdom.

Grant us now the wisdom to use these gifts wisely, knowing that what we do is for Your glory, not ours. Make us aware of the true needs of Your Church and help us to address them. In this time of prosperity, keep us from relying more on finances than we do on You. Keep us all pointed in the same direction, that of extending Your kingdom both inwardly and outwardly.

Thank You, Lord, for the bountiful blessings you have given to Your people in this place. This we pray in Jesus' name. Amen.

FOR THE SUCCESSFUL RECOVERY OF A GROUP MEMBER

Dear Lord Jesus, thank You for hearing the prayers of Your servants and healing _____ of (his/her) illness. We especially praise You for returning our (brother/sister) to us to continue the work we have begun. Give to _____ the renewed strength of body and spirit to continue to serve You and Your people. Grant that this sickness may not return, but that _____ may continue to improve in physical and spiritual strength.

We praise You, O Lord, for Your goodness to Your servants. Continue to bless us with Your presence as You have in the past. Through Christ, our Lord. Amen.

PRAYERS FOR THE CLOSING OF A MEETING

Gracious Lord, in this closing hour, we thank and praise You for Your presence. We ask Your forgiveness for those things that we have said and done that did not glorify You or help Your people. Heal the wounds inflicted by pride and restore our enthusiasm for Your work. According to Your will, bring to completion the plans we have made and the assignments given.

Give to each of us Your protection from accident as well as from the temptations of Satan. Guide and protect us all until we meet again in this place or in Your place. In Jesus' name. Amen.

Dear Father, as we close this meeting we thank You for blessing us with Your presence and filling us with Your Spirit. We especially thank You for enabling us to complete the work set before us. We pray now that You would bless our efforts according to Your will and bring to a stronger faith those whom we serve.

Protect each of us as we go our separate ways, sending Your holy angels to attend us. Help us to be Your presence in a cold and dark world. Hear us for Jesus' sake. Amen.

BASED ON LUTHER'S EVENING PRAYER

We thank You, our heavenly Father, through Jesus Christ, our dear Lord, that You have brought us to the end of this time of meeting and fellowship. We ask You to forgive us where we have strayed from Your paths, and graciously restore us to paths that are right.

For into Your hands we now give ourselves, our bodies and souls and all that is dear to us. Send Your holy angels to protect us, that Satan may not have opportunity to harm us in body or in soul. Make us truly one with You, through Christ, our Lord. Amen.

BASED ON THE APOSTOLIC BENEDICTION

Almighty God, we thank You for demonstrating to us how much You love us, as we have been reminded of Your grace in Christ. Wherever we go, help us to spread Your love to those who need it.

Lord Jesus, we thank You for Your grace and blessing as we have experienced it during this time of meeting. Be with us now as we part, so we may share Your grace with others.

Enlightening Spirit, we thank You for the warmth of Christian fellowship that we have experienced. Fill us with Your gifts that we may truly give to those to whom You lead us.

Praise be to You, O blessed Trinity. In the name of the Father and of the Son and of the Holy Spirit. Amen.

THE LORD'S PRAYER

To be used responsively) The entire group is to say the parts in uppercase/bold; either an individual or individuals in rotation may say the intervening parts.

OUR FATHER, WHO ART IN HEAVEN:

You, dear Lord, are our heavenly Father through the adoption earned for us by Jesus Christ, Your Son, our Lord.

HALLOWED BE YOUR NAME:

We pray that in all of our activities, we do nothing to violate the family name we were given at our baptisms.

YOUR KINGDOM COME:

As You have brought us into Your kingdom, help us, wherever we are, to bring the good news of the saving grace of Your love to others.

YOUR WILL BE DONE ON EARTH AS IT IS IN HEAVEN:

Bend us, O Lord, to Your ways of doing things, just as Your holy angels do in serving You.

GIVE US THIS DAY OUR DAILY BREAD:

We thank You for giving us just what we need, when we need it. Help us to look only to You for our daily needs, not to our own resources.

FORGIVE US OUR TRESPASSES AS WE FORGIVE THOSE WHO TRESPASS AGAINST US:

Forgive us, dear Father, our many sins that separate us from You. Strengthen us to forgive the sins of others that separate us from them.

AND LEAD US NOT INTO TEMPTATION:

O Lord, keep us from our adversary, the devil. Enable us to recognize his evil devices and strengthen us to flee from them.

BUT DELIVER US FROM EVIL:

Free us, dear Savior, from all that would hinder Your work. Send Your holy angels to accompany us on our way.

FOR YOURS IS THE KINGDOM AND THE POWER AND THE GLORY FOREVER AND EVER. AMEN.

To You, O Lord, be praise and thanksgiving for ordaining our new life in Your kingdom and for sending the power of Your Spirit into our lives to the glory of Your holy name, through Christ, our Lord. Amen.

TOPICAL INDEX

SCRIPTURE INDEX